instructional
implications
of inquiry

instructional
implications
of inquiry

Frank L. Ryan

University of California, Riverside

Arthur K. Ellis

University of Minnesota

21478

Prentice-Hall, Inc., *Englewood Cliffs, New Jersey*

Library of Congress Cataloging in Publication Data

RYAN, FRANK L.
　Instructional implications of inquiry.

　(Curriculum and teaching)
　Includes bibliographical references.
　1. Study, Method of.　2. Research.　3. Report
writing.　4. Social sciences—Study and teaching.
I. Ellis, Arthur K., joint author.　II. Title.
LB1049.R92 1974　　　372.8′3′044　　　73-22430
ISBN 0-13-467829-X
ISBN 0-13-467811-7 (pbk.)

© 1974 by PRENTICE-HALL, INC., Englewood Cliffs, N.J.

Printed in the United States of America

10　9　8　7　6　5　4　3　2　1

Prentice-Hall International, Inc., *London*
Prentice-Hall of Australia, Pty. Ltd., *Sydney*
Prentice-Hall of Canada, Ltd., *Toronto*
Prentice-Hall of India Private Limited, *New Delhi*
Prentice-Hall of Japan, Inc., *Tokyo*

contents

preface

One of the persistent, significant characteristics of recent curricular developments has been the establishment of the idea that students should not only continue to be exposed to the knowledge produced by others but should also directly experience generating knowledge—that is, they should become inquirers. The basic definition of inquiry which we use in this book is the activity of working with data and making statements from data. Through the activities of inquiry, investigators—whether they identify with the social, natural, physical, or mathematical sciences—generate knowledge.

The instructional proposal that students question, analyze, and even generate knowledge, as well as receive it, is extremely difficult for many teachers to implement if they themselves have never been cast in an inquiring role during their formal educational experience. Therefore, we have chosen to interweave two basic strands throughout the book, which, when stated in question form, become: What are the characteristics of inquiry and its operations? What are the implications of inquiry for the classroom?

The book is intended for anyone, regardless of grade level interest or subject matter interest, who wants to learn about inquiry and its instructional implications, even though the majority of the examples presented are oriented toward social studies instruction. We contend that all students, regardless of the categorical titles we impose on them (first grader, twelfth grader, road runner, third tracker), can be inquirers in a way that is consistent and compatible with the activity of that select group of inquirers currently extending the frontiers of knowledge. And, in response to the anticipated question, not only *can* students of all ages be inquirers, but we believe there are excellent reasons why they *should* be inquirers.

We have chosen to use a wide range of inquiry examples, some of which we have pursued from their inception to a conclusion. Other examples are treated in a more cursory fashion. We hope that by including both, we have served your need to learn about inquiry procedures as well as your age level and subject matter interests. In several instances, we refer to such statistical techniques as chi-square, t-test, and analysis of variance, and how they may be used in inquiry activities. While readers who have some background in the use of these and other statistics may find this discussion useful, we wish to stress that the reader needs no statistical background to comprehend the spirit of the activities.

Our experiences repeatedly suggest that an excellent strategy for learning about inquiry is to involve the learner actively as an inquirer. Certainly, textbooks on inquiry need not provide the strategic exception; they should instead be viable models for the instructional implementation of inquiry activities. Therefore, within the format of this book, we have extended an invitation to you to participate actively as an inquirer. We hope that through such involvement you will concurrently establish the spirit, attitudes, and operational characteristics of inquiry, from which you can draw when you want to make instructional applications with your students.

To facilitate your instructional efforts, we have described more than seventy-five specific activities for inquiry applications to the classroom. Sixty-one of these ideas are found in the instructional implications sections of Chapters 2 through 7. The remaining ideas occur in the main presentations of the various chapters. A special index for all of the ideas begins on page 151.

*instructional
implications
of inquiry*

prologue:
what is inquiry?

At a team meeting early in the school year, three teachers were discussing how to help their students gain a perspective on the changes that had come about in social studies teaching over the years. They hit upon the idea of having students learn how social studies were taught during the 1950s, so that the students could compare the methods used in the '50s and the '70s. The teachers felt that the students would be surprised at the changes that had occurred over two decades. As the meeting ended, the three teachers decided that each would bring to the next meeting a plan of action for teaching the idea.

Let's sit in on the next meeting:

Ms. Olsen: I had the custodian let me into the storeroom where old materials are kept. I found dozens of old textbooks and teachers' lesson plans from the 1950s. I'm going to have my students look through them and reach conclusions about what social studies classes were like then.

Mr. Hammersmith: I remembered some curriculum books I had in education classes at State U. In one book on the history of education, part of a chapter was devoted to social studies methods before the new social studies came about. The author explained exactly how it was then. I'm making ditto copies of that excerpt for my students to read. Also, I'm preparing a lecture which I will call "Social Studies Yesterday and Today: Where Have We Come From—Where Are We Now?"

Mr. LaMere: I decided that one way for the students to find out is to ask the people who were involved. I'm going to have them interview former students and teachers from the 1950s. If they find enough people, they should be able to piece together a pretty accurate picture of social studies in those days.

Which of these teachers are using inquiry methods; that is, which teachers are giving their students an opportunity to personally generate (rather than merely receive) knowledge about social studies in the 1950s? Answer "yes" or "no" beside each name and briefly defend your answer.

Ms. Olsen: _____

_____

_____

Mr. Hammersmith: _____

_____

_____

Mr. LaMere: _____

_____

_____

Without knowing any more than we do about the three proposed learning environments, we would say that Ms. Olsen and Mr. LaMere are planning inquiry experiences for their students while Mr. Hammersmith is not. The basic difference among the three teachers lies in how the students are to arrive at the product, knowledge of social studies classes in the 1950s. Ms. Olsen and Mr. LaMere propose that their students work with data to make inferences. Mr. Hammersmith proposes to present his students with conclusions.

1

why involve students
in inquiry activities?

Perhaps it is best to begin a book on inquiry teaching strategies with a few statements about inquiry. Let us pose a series of statements about inquiry to which you may respond "yes" or "no." After you have defined a position on inquiry by virtue of your responses, check them against ours. If we are in complete agreement, then not only will this book tend to reinforce your biases, but it may also expand your ideas about the possibilities inherent in inquiry teaching. If we agree less than completely, we invite you to read the book in a spirit of healthy skepticism—we may even convince you of the validity of some of our ideas.

We perceive one immediate limitation of the medium you have before you: you are limited to learning from a book. To establish and support an environment of free and open inquiry, you, as well as we, should have the opportunity to express ideas. We have attempted to create such an environment by varying the textual style from pure exposition, but at best, the result is less than optimum.

STATEMENTS ABOUT INQUIRY (circle yes or no)

1. Yes   No   Younger as well as older children are capable of carrying on research in much the same manner as a social scientist.

2. Yes   No   Inquiry learning is less efficient than traditional forms of learning.

3. Yes   No   Inquiry teaching, like many other ideas in education, is a fad that will pass away in time.

4. Yes   No   Inquiry teaching often fails because teachers lack sufficient background in its techniques.

5. Yes   No   Such concepts as "data" and "inference" are too sophisticated to be dealt with realistically in the schools.

6. Yes   No   Typical textbooks are often an obstruction to inquiry learning.

This is how we answered the questions:

1. *Yes.* Obviously they have neither the formal training nor the resources of the social scientist. However, we believe that with proper guidance they can pose problems, gather and process data, and reach conclusions in much the same manner as the scientist.

2. *No.* Inquiry learning may erode the time devoted to such traditional coverage as "all fifty states" or "450 years in nine months," but there is no reason to assume that the inquirer is learning less than the student in a traditional classroom.

3. *No.* This answer, like the others, is strictly an opinion. However, if inquiry learning represents an attempt to simulate the scientific investigation of problems, then it would seem unfortunate for the schools to abandon a model of learning accepted by those who actually generate the knowledge we learn.

4. *Yes.* We think that teachers are seldom given sufficient systematic exposure to the operations of inquiry to enable them to make meaningful instructional applications with students. This book attempts to expose you to inquiry operations so that you can make a successful start in that direction.

5. *No.* The concepts of "data" and "inference" are basic to the operations of inquiry. While some may find the terms themselves confusing, at least initially, our own experience with students of all ages tells us that they are very capable of gathering and processing data and making inferences.

6. *Yes.* Although certain improvements have recently been made in text-books, the central function of a textbook remains that of imparting existing information to learners. This is acceptable. The danger lies in the ever-present tendency of teachers to perceive the textbook as something that must be covered, rather than as simply another data source.

You may already have written us off as being wrong. Are you sure you have enough data for your inference? Even if your response is "yes" (and we find it difficult to grasp how it could be), we ask you to adopt one of the requisite attitudes for anyone participating in inquiry activities—open-mindedness to others' ideas, even if they conflict with your own. We simply ask for a hearing, so that even if you eventually reject our ideas, at least you will know what you are rejecting. It is our strong conviction, however, that the operations of inquiry can be translated into valid learning experiences for students of all ages, and that teachers involved in inquiry can significantly enhance their present repertoire of teaching strategies.

The Idea of Structure in Inquiry

Certain subjects in the curriculum derive their subject matter and, hopefully, their methodology from scholarly parent disciplines. Social studies draws on the accumulated knowledge, ideas, and procedures of anthropology, cultural geography, economics, history, political science, social psychology, and sociology. These disciplines all study social phenomena. The essence of social studies, then, is inquiry into man's behavior: *How* does man behave (in varying circumstances throughout time and across space)? *Why* does he behave as he does? *What* alternative form of behavior might be posed? Similarly, new science curricula are based on the structures of the natural sciences—biology, physics, chemistry, geology, and astronomy. The essence of natural science is inquiry into the attributes and behavior of so-called natural phenomena.

Each of the sciences listed above has a twofold structure composed of (1) its procedures or methods of inquiry (for example, the way or ways in which an anthropologist goes about studying a particular culture), and (2) its main ideas and major concepts (for example, the concept of culture, with its attendant subconcepts of acculturation, innovation, tradition, enculturation). The first facet of structure is concerned with the *process* of scientific investigation, the second, with the *products* of investigation. Current and emerging social studies curriculum philosophy emphasizes that students should become involved in investigating problems in much the same fashion as the social scientist, to develop key concepts and processes. In this regard, the structures of the social sciences form a framework for the social studies, and the structures of the natural sciences form a framework for school science.

Too often, however, the content area of the social studies has involved only fact gathering about places, people, and events. Students of the geography of the United States are required to memorize capital cities and crops. Students of current events are asked to name world leaders. Students of the past are required to remember the dates of major battles and discoveries. The problem with information of this sort is that it is potentially trivial, often disjointed, and lacking in transfer value.

Fact-centered, nonconceptual learning encourages the student to assume a passive role, dependent on teacher or textbook cues for information. His task is to remember what the teacher or textbook stresses, regardless of whether particular facts or pieces of information are related or sequenced in any fashion. The learner never questions material presented by such authoritative sources as textbooks and teachers. Why would the student question that George Washington was the first president of the United States, or that cotton is a major crop of the South? Obviously, a fact-centered mode of learning runs counter to the nature of scientific inquiry.

Of course, a fact-centered curriculum offers both teacher and student a certain amount of security. "Progress" is easily measured in terms of right and wrong answers to questions, predictability of readings and discussions, and letter grades for assignments and report cards. The world of school learning is made simple—and uninspiring.

Consider the following example of social studies learning: "Huetar are located along the lower slopes of the Talamanca Range." If you have no conceptual background of information, you will undoubtedly perceive this bit of information as meaningless and trivial. "What are huetar?" you ask. "Trees, rodents, a primitive tribe? Where is the Talamanca Range?" Yet this is verifiable information that can be memorized and repeated in written or oral form without any concept development having occurred. Knowing this piece of "truth" could even help you answer a test item correctly. If this example seems far-fetched to you as a teacher, consider the plight of the eight- or ten-year-old who must continually memorize information no less obscure to him. Even students who do well on tests and often answer questions in class find that they remember very little of what they have learned from one year to the next.

Traditionally, educators have been content to skim off the results of others' scholarly investigations and force-feed them to learners. Now, knowledge of the products of the investigations of others is still required, but so is an understanding of how the products are generated. Inquiry teaching is a direct response to the concern that learners understand the characteristics of knowledge and how it comes about.

An alternative to a product-centered curriculum is one which places primary emphasis on a high degree of inquiry-related student involvement. Involvement-learning possesses more staying power than fact-centered learning, because it can be applied in a wider variety of situations and it does not become irrelevant or dated. The operations of scientific inquiry have a transfer value that validates their use in the many unforeseen circumstances each learner will encounter throughout his life. For example, the student who has learned to categorize and label is much better equipped to analyze a future problem than the student who has been denied the opportunity to use these processes.

Today the only certainty is that things will change. Indeed, the rate at which things change appears certain to accelerate. Alvin Toffler, in *Future Shock,* describes the "fantastic intrusion of novelty or newness into our existence." [1] He maintains that "to survive . . . the individual must become infinitely more adaptable and capable than before." [2] In our era of knowledge explosion, urbanization, women's liberation, greatly expanded means of communication and transportation, modification of the traditional family structure, breakthroughs in medical science, and even some changes in teaching methods, the scope and pace of social and technological change are dizzying. The students who are in school today may experience, and even help to bring about, such changes as a greatly increased life span, communication with life in other parts of the universe, a widening or narrowing of the gap between rich and poor, and radically different means of societal organization.

Because of the great proliferation of knowledge during the past decade, it is crucial that students be taught the skills which will facilitate independent and cooperative analysis of problems, and that they attain a knowledge of man's behavior which goes beyond the mere memorization of factual information. To accomplish this, it seems advisable that they become actively involved in such investigative operations as defining problems, making hypotheses, gathering and processing data, and making inferences.

The two examples that follow are designed to illustrate the notion that students can operate as inquirers at a conceptual level by simulating the role of the scientific inquirer.

Paul Brandwein describes a lesson in which first graders explore the generalization, "People everywhere are governed by commonly accepted

---

[1] Alvin Toffler, *Future Shock* (New York: Random House, Inc., 1970), p. 29.
[2] Ibid., p. 30.

rules." [3] To help them understand that generalization as it applies to the concept of norms of behavior, the teacher asks primary-grade children to collect data on their nightly bedtimes. By taking home a dittoed form for his parents to complete, the child becomes in effect a social scientist engaged in gathering data which will help explain man's behavior. Thus, the learner becomes an active inquirer rather than a mere recipient of information.

When the children have returned the bedtime data to class, the teacher is ready to help them establish a norm for their classroom. Suppose six children go to bed at eight o'clock, seven at eight-thirty, six at nine o'clock, and two whenever they choose. A norm for the class (eight to nine o'clock) has been established.

Now the children may wish to poll other primary students or even children in the fourth or fifth grade. Older children will undoubtedly have a later bedtime norm. This discovery might serve as the focal point of a discussion in which the children attempt to account for the difference in bedtime norms. In addition, the teacher may wish to probe: "Why do you go to bed when you do?" The many answers will no doubt reflect divergent points of view. With the teacher's help, the children can discuss reasons for having bedtime rules and other rules. They might wish to inquire into other norms of behavior such as mealtimes, play habits, and household chores. In further pursuit of this idea, the children could compare and contrast a cultural norm (bedtime) with more formalized norms such as traffic laws. In accordance with the idea we expressed earlier—that the structures of the social science disciplines be used to guide students' social studies experiences—the children in this lesson were involved in several operations of inquiry (data gathering and inferring) leading to the development of a social science concept (norms of behavior). The skills to which they were introduced are basic to scholarly investigation, retaining their validity in future inquiry into human behavior.

At a higher grade level, a student inquiring into the concept of enculturation, or the way in which a person grows up in a society, might use the data-gathering techniques of participant observation and interviewing to help answer the inquiry question, "How do first-grade children spend their playtime?" As an investigator, the student might interview two or three first-graders, asking questions such as, "When you can do whatever you choose, what do you like to do?" and "When your school friends come to play at your house, what do you do? Responses to these and other questions will help him in his data gathering. As a further means of determining what he needs to know, our student-anthropologist will observe the inter-

---

[3] Paul F. Brandwein, *Toward a Discipline of Responsible Consent* (New York: Harcourt Brace Jovanovich, Inc., 1969), pp. 36–37.

viewees at play. He thus becomes a participant observer, spending time with his subjects and taking field notes.

Compiling and writing up his field notes in the form of a report, the student-anthropologst may ultimately want to make some interpretive or inferential statements addressed to the questions, "What does the playtime behavior of these children mean?" and "How does their playtime behavior reflect the values of their society?" As he writes his report, he must be aware that as an interviewer and participant observer, he himself may affect both the children's answers to questions and their playtime behavior.

In both the norms-of-behavior and the enculturation examples, students are involved in concept development in an active, investigative mode. In both instances, they engage in observing, recording, and communicating human behavior. Their task (at least implicitly) is to answer the questions, How does man behave? Why does he behave as he does? What alternative forms of behavior might be posed?

Many curricular areas, especially science and the social studies, are attractive to students who in most cases are only too eager to learn about the world in which they live. The key to encouraging those students lies in the teaching-learning strategies used inside and outside the classroom. Teachers must create the kinds of situations in which their students are actively involved in systematic process and concept development.

The final chapter of this book includes a continuance of the theme, "Why inquiry?" You may want to glance at it before going on to Chapter 2.

2

stating a problem and hypothesizing

The most basic step in inquiry is formulating a problem or question to structure the investigation. In addition, the problem serves as the key to the inquiry activity that develops during the investigation. In this respect, the problem controls the investigation and keeps it from straying off-course. The problem functions as the stage-setting device in the investigative process, and the question of whether an investigation will be worthwhile depends on the statement of the problem.

Stating Problems That Lead to Inquiry

To gain a concrete idea of the control exerted by the problem on the investigation, consider the following example:

An investigator states that his inquiry will be directed to the problem of determining the capital city of Nebraska in the year 1972.

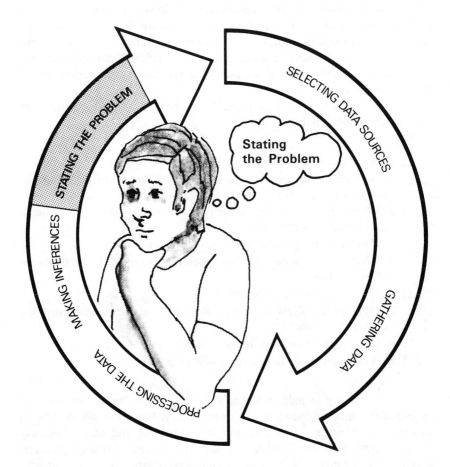

Figure 1   Inquiry operations: stating the problem and making hypotheses

While we may be stretching the point to call the pursuit of such a problem "inquiry," let us follow our investigator as he seeks the answer. He turns to volume "N" of the encyclopedia and finds that Lincoln is the capital city. His investigation ends.

In one regard, this was a successful investigation. The learner stated a problem and answered it definitively. However, because the problem controls the conduct of the inquiry, we should pose problems that have the potential to lead us beyond recall or looking up the "correct" answer.

For contrast, consider this problem:

What effects does the application of gibberellic acid have on the growth of beans and peas?

Obviously, the answer to this problem could be looked up and the question treated at the recall level. An alternative procedure, however, is the possibility of a controlled experiment involving several plants to which the acid is applied and others to which it is not. Specifically, this problem will encourage the development of such skills as systematic observation, record keeping, predicting, and verifying.

Some problems follow. Place a check ($\sqrt{}$) beside those which you think offer potential for inquiry.

_____ 1. Who discovered America?

_____ 2. How do the members of the Chamber of Commerce feel about the new sports stadium proposal?

_____ 3. What is the relationship between the extent of a person's formal education and his occupation?

_____ 4. How many people voted for Mayor Black in 1972?

_____ 5. What changes in rural land-use occurred in Dakota County between 1940 and 1964?

_____ 6. What is the future of the world?

_____ 7. What are the effects on spelling achievement of intermittent distraction during study time?

_____ 8. How old is the president of the United States?

_____ 9. Which color is more beautiful: blue or green?

Instead of trying to judge whether you checked the "right" answers, we choose at this time to discuss the spirit of inquiry. Inquiry is *not* looking up someone else's predetermined answer to a problem and unquestioningly accepting it as the truth. Neither is inquiry the process of posing questions which cannot be answered because they are overly large in scope or strictly a matter of opinion. Inquiry implies an active investigation on the part of the learner, who consults numerous sources to help him reach his conclusion. Inquiry implies experimentation; the investigator controls a situation in order to deal objectively with various relationships. Inquiry implies the use of such processes as observing, measuring, recording, and hypothesizing. Inquiry implies gathering data and making inferences from those data.

Making Hypotheses

Investigators set the stage for their inquiry by stating one or more hypotheses, educated guesses made in advance of an investigation as a means of preventing it from straying beyond its purpose.[1] The hypothesis is actually a prediction of the result of the investigation, and the findings will tend either to support the hypothesis or to raise doubts about it.

In formulating hypotheses, the investigator draws on any data that are available, accessible, and relevant. The first grader might hypothesize that most first graders go to bed at 8:00 (because he or she does). Such a hypothesis would be eitheir supported or unsupported by the data the first grader gathers.

INVOLVING YOU IN STATING RESEARCHABLE HYPOTHESES

Here is a hypothesis stated by Marvin, who will now begin his investigation: "People are extremely friendly." Marvin's hypothesis is (check one or more):

_____ 1. too specific.

_____ 2. too general.

_____ 3. hardly researchable.

_____ 4. overly scientific.

Marvin's hypothesis is too general and hardly researchable because it fails to state any conditions and breaks down in definition. (What, for example, does "extremely friendly" mean?)

Examine the following two problems and try to state hypotheses about them.

1. What are the attitudes of the people of Foxborough toward pay television?

Hypothesis: _____

[1] In Chapter 1 we chided those of you who made the "inference" that we were "wrong" in our hopes for inquiry teaching. However, this does not preclude the possibility that you have sufficient data from your teaching experience to treat the statement about our being "wrong" as a hypothesis.

2. What effect, if any, has the Smith-Johnson method of teaching driving safety on students' attitudes toward driver education?

Hypothesis: _____

_____

For #1 you might have made one of the following hypotheses:

A majority of the people of Foxborough favor pay television.

A majority of the people of Foxborough oppose pay television.

A majority of the people of Foxborough have no opinion on the issue of pay television.

For #2 you might have made one of the following hypotheses:

The Smith-Johnson method has a positive effect on students' attitudes toward driver education.

The Smith-Johnson method has a negative effect on students' attitudes toward driver education.

The Smith-Johnson method has no effect on students' attitudes toward driver education.

At this point let us take up the idea of refining a problem and stating a hypothesis about it. Consider this problem: Which of the three routes shown in Figure 2 is the best way to drive from A to B? (Check one.)

_____ Dry Gulch Road
_____ Interstate 422
_____ Skyview Drive
_____ can't say

We checked "can't say" because our problem needs refinement. For example, what do we mean by "the best way"? The safest way? The fastest

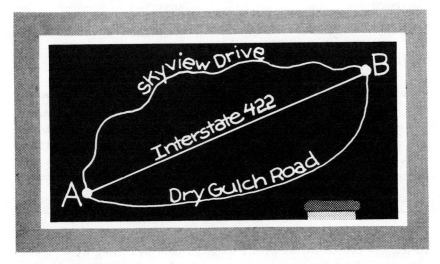

Figure 2 A source for hypothesizing on the driving times between two points

way? The most scenic way? What, after all, do we want to know about the problem?

Let's focus the problem: assume that we want to know the fastest way to drive from A to B. This leads us to the next step in our investigation— stating a hypothesis about the question. This educated guess is developed from the information we are able to gather before we actually conduct the investigation. Of course, if we could predict with 100 percent certainty the outcome of an investigation, there would be no need to conduct it. But because most of us have lesser powers of insight, we hypothesize (guess) toward our prediction of the logical outcome.

Examine Figure 2 for clues and try to hypothesize the outcome of the investigation directed toward determining the fastest way to drive from A to B. Which of the following hypotheses do you choose (check one), and why do you choose it? Provide reasons.

HYPOTHESES   REASONS

_____ 1. The fastest way to drive from   _____
          A to B is via Dry Gulch   _____
          Road.   _____

_____ 2. The fastest way to drive from   _____
          A to B is via Interstate 422.   _____

                                             _____

HYPOTHESES	REASONS
_____ 3. The fastest way to drive from A to B is via Skyview Drive.	_____
	_____
	_____

We hypothesize that Interstate 422 is the fastest way from A to B. Our reasons are based on the observations that (1) it is the shortest distance between the two points, (2) it is the straightest of the three routes, and (3) it probably has a higher speed limit because it is an interstate highway.

To test our hypothesis, we decide to gather data by driving from A to B three times via each route and averaging the driving times for each route. Next we process our data by developing a chart shown in Table 1.

Table 1   Average driving times from Point A to Point B via three routes

Route	First Run	Second Run	Third Run	Average Driving Time
Dry Gulch Road	30 min.	35 min.	31 min.	32 min.
Interstate 422	22 min.	24 min.	23 min.	23 min.
Skyview Drive	42 min.	40 min.	41 min.	41 min.

At this point, we examine our processed data and make a decision about the support, or lack of it, for our hypothesis. On the basis of our results, we decide we have (check one):

_____ supported our hypothesis.
_____ failed to support our hypothesis.

The data supported our hypothesis, because Interstate 422 yielded the fastest average time. We have purposely used the term *support* rather than *prove*. Knowledge is often very tentative, especially in the area of human behavior. Thus, we state a hypothesis, do our research, and limit ourselves to statements of support or nonsupport for the hypothesis, rather than saying (less humbly) that we have proved something.

Some problems stated as questions follow. For each problem, check the statement which could be a fruitful hypothesis for that problem.

1. How do members of the Chamber of Commerce feel about the new sports stadium proposal?

HYPOTHESES

_____ a. The members of the Chamber of Commerce favor the new sports stadium proposal.

_____ b. The members of the Chamber of Commerce are wealthy.

_____ c. The members of the Chamber of Commerce always act in the best interest of the city.

2. What is the relationship between the extent of a person's formal education and his occupation?

HYPOTHESES

_____ a. Some people are denied a formal education by circumstance.

_____ b. There is a positive relationship between the extent of a person's formal education and his occupation.

_____ c. Most people are satisfied with their present occupation.

3. What are the effects on spelling achievement of intermittent distraction during study time?

HYPOTHESES

_____ a. Distraction is related to spelling achievement.

_____ b. Distraction affects spelling achievement.

_____ c. Distraction has a negative effect on spelling achievement.

We think that an appropriate answer for #1 is "a." The other two hypotheses, although interesting, are not germane to the question, and therefore fail to provide guideposts for gathering and processing the data.

Our answer for #2 is "b." Neither "a" nor "c" helps answer the question. Our answer for #3 is "c." Both "a" and "b" pertain to the question, but they lack specifics. Hypothesis "a" postulates a relationship, but we don't know what form it might take. Hypothesis "b" postulates an effect, but we don't know whether it might be positive or negative.

By now you may have discovered some guidelines for stating problems and hypotheses. Place a check next to the statements below which you think exemplify the rules or procedures an investigator should remember at the initial phase of an investigation.

_____ 1. The problem should pose at least three hypotheses.

_____ 2. The problem should be one that can be answered by gathering data.

_____ 3. The problem should be stated clearly, with terms defined if necessary.

_____ 4. The problem should be further refined by the statement of a hypothesis (hypotheses).

_____ 5. The hypothesis (hypotheses) should be based on a rationale.

_____ 6. The problem should not be beyond the scope of the investigator's resources.

=====

We checked #2, #3, #4, #5, and #6. If you want to review our reasoning, glance quickly through the chapter once more. In summary, our list of criteria include the following:

1. The problem must be one that can be answered by gathering data.
2. The problem should be stated clearly, with terms defined if necessary.
3. The problem should be further refined by the statement of a hypothesis (hypotheses).
4. The question or hypothesis (hypotheses) should be based on a rationale.
5. The problem should not be beyond the scope of the investigator's resources.

Summary

Our control point has been the cruciality of the problem statement as a guide to the conduct of a systematic investigation. The problem must be stated so that it is unambiguous. It must also lead the inquirer to go beyond looking up the "right" answer. A problem is sometimes stated as a hypothesis, or educated guess, and sometimes posed as a question. In either case, the inquirer, after stating his problem, becomes actively involved in gathering data, processing data, and making inferences.

Instructional Implications

As you read this chapter on stating problems and hypotheses, you may have been thinking that this type of activity bears at best remote resemblance to any classroom instructional situation with which you are familiar. We suggest that you consider the ideas presented in this chapter and developed more fully in subsequent chapters as having direct implications for classroom use with students from primary through secondary levels.

Imagine that the different types of learning possible in a school setting at any age level are arranged on a continuum. Learning varies from memory work at a very low level with little student involvement to the creation of new knowledge at a very high level with greater student involvement.

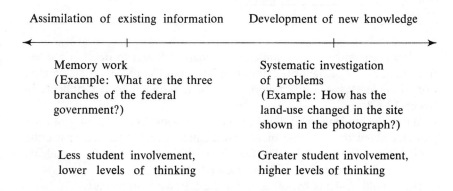

Assimilation of existing information   Development of new knowledge

Memory work (Example: What are the three branches of the federal government?)	Systematic investigation of problems (Example: How has the land-use changed in the site shown in the photograph?)
Less student involvement, lower levels of thinking	Greater student involvement, higher levels of thinking

It seems reasonable that students memorize some information. It also seems reasonable that they assimilate some measure of existing information through books, films, lectures, and discussion. But just as certainly, it seems reasonable that they help create information by doing the things that scientific investigators do: posing problems and hypotheses, selecting data sources, gathering and processing data, and making inferences. We think it follows that, having played the role of investigator, a student may be in a more viable position to deal rationally with conclusions presented in textbooks and with inferences made by speakers. Such a student may begin to question: "What sources of information did you use? How reliable are your sources? How were you able to make such an inference?"

The purpose of the following activity is to give your students an opportunity to pose research-oriented questions and hypotheses. You may find it useful to present the activity to your students as a prototype exercise in scientific investigation. Because you have read only the beginning of this book, you may have reservations about the thoroughness of your knowledge of research methods. At this point, however, you need not worry about whether the students actually conduct the investigation. If they do, make some notes about the procedures they use to test the hypotheses and decide whether you want to refine them as you read further.

1. Give each student a copy of a chart similar to the one shown in Table 2, and ask him to complete it. Younger children can state their preferences orally.

Table 2   Sample questionnaire

Write Your Favorite:

TV progam _____	Name _____
Car _____	Sex _____
Sport _____	Grade _____
Recreation activity _____	Age _____
Color _____	
Subject _____	

After each student has completed his chart, ask him to develop a question about any of his favorite things that he would like to ask his classmates. For example: What is the favorite television program of the students in Room 12-C?

When the students have finished their questions, ask them to write hypotheses about the outcome of an investigation directed toward answering the questions. For example: The favorite television program of the students in Room 12-C is the Skip Williams Comedy Hour.

How could students hypothesize for the following problems?

Do boys have a greater preference for sports cars than girls?

At what age do students most prefer baseball?

What is the favorite recreational activity of the students in the class?

Are age and color preference related?

Do boys prefer different subjects from girls?

Other potential questions for hypothesizing include:

What are the favorite subjects of students in our class?

Which team will win the World Series?

Do boys or girls run faster?

Are boys or girls better spellers?

At what age do our students feel dating should begin?

Should the United States give military aid to dictatorships?

How do our students feel about the question of world government?

2. You might try the following investigation with your students as an exercise in developing a hypothesis. At the conclusion of their inquiry into the question, "Did the Chinese really discover America?" students should be encouraged to share their hypotheses with each other. Even though the students have spent a considerable amount of time dealing with the question, their conclusions should be treated as hypotheses in this case because of the slight amount of evidence presented.

After the students have read the following excerpt and studied a map showing the directional flow of the Japan Current, ask them to make preliminary hypotheses by indicating on the continuum below their feelings at this point.

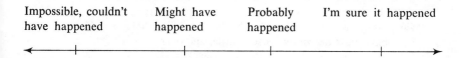

Impossible, couldn't   Might have   Probably   I'm sure it happened
have happened   happened   happened

Now divide them into small groups and give each group a shuffled set of white cards and a shuffled set of gray cards. Ask them to match white and gray cards to build a data base from which to refine or revise their earlier hypotheses.

Did the Chinese Discover America in 458 A.D.? [2]

In 458 A.D., five men supposedly set sail from China. Following the Japan Current, they traveled 20,000 li eastward. Twenty thousand li equals about 7,000 miles. [Students refer to a map of the Japan Current in an encyclopedia, atlas, or geography book].

Sometime during the same year, the five travelers reached a land which they called Fusang. It is where Mexico can be found today. They are supposed to have stayed there for forty years. In 499 A.D. they returned to China.

When they returned, one of them, Hwui Shan, told the emperor about their adventures in the New World. A servant of the emperor wrote down Hwui Shan's story. We still have that story. Some scholars who have read

[2] Adapted from *Inquiring About American History*, W. R. Fielder, ed. (Holt, Rinehart and Winston, 1972, pp. 23–27. Used with permission.)

it believe it can be used to prove that Hwui Shan and his friends discovered the New World in 458 A.D.—more than 1,000 years before Columbus.

As you read part of Hwui Shan's story, ask yourself if you agree with those scholars. Try to decide whether it was possible or probable that the Chinese reached America before the Vikings or Columbus.

Hwui Shan's Story

Fusang is located 20,000 li east of the country of Ta Han in China. The Land of Marked Bodies is 7,000 li northwest of Japan. Its people have marks or stripes on their bodies like wild animals. In front they have three marks. If the marks are large and straight, they belong to the upper class, but if the marks are small and crooked, they belong to the lower class.

The land of Fusang has many Fusang trees, which give it its name. The Fusang tree's leaves look like those of the T'ung tree in China. Its first sprouts are like bamboo shoots. The people of the country eat these sprouts. Their fruit is like a pear but reddish. The people also spin thread from the bark. They use the thread to make coarse cloth from which they make their clothing. They also make a finer fabric from this thread. The wood of the Fusang tree is used to build houses, and the bark is used to make paper.

The people of Fusang have a system of writing. But they have no forts or walled cities, no military weapons or soldiers. They do not wage war.

Their ground has no iron, but it has copper. They have large cattle horns which they use as containers. The largest horns hold about five gallons. They have carts drawn by horses, cattle, and deer.

The Land of Women

The Land of Women is about 1,000 li beyond the Land of Fusang. Its women are completely covered with hair. They walk standing up straight, and chatter a lot among themselves. They are shy when they see ordinary people. Their babies are able to walk when they are one hundred days old, and they are fully grown in three or four years.

(Hwui Shan also gave the Chinese emperor a kind of stone which was almost transparent. It was about a foot around and made in the form of a mirror.)

Gray Cards	White Cards
1. Hwui Shan said he traveled east 20,000 li from China.	1,000 li = about 333 miles 20,000 li = about 7,000 miles Mexico via the Japan Current is about 7,000 miles from China.
2. The Land of Marked Bodies was 7,000 li from Japan.	Marked women lived at Point Barrow, Alaska, about 2,400 miles from Japan.

Gray Cards	White Cards
3. Fusang has copper but no iron. The people there also have a system of writing.	Archeologists have found that Mexican Indians used copper by 400 A.D. Spanish explorers discovered iron in Mexico after 1500 A.D. By 400 A.D. some Indians in Mexico had a system of writing.
4. The people of Fusang had large cattle horns.	Scholars knew that Montezuma, the Aztec chief of Mexico, showed Cortez, the Spanish explorer, some large bison horns after 1500 A.D.
5. The Land of Women is 1,000 li beyond Fusang.	Central American monkeys live about 300 miles south of Mexico. These monkeys are shy, chattering, and hairy.
6. The Land of Fusang is named after the Fusang trees, which have a reddish, pearlike fruit. Sprouts of the Fusang trees look like bamboo.	"Mexico" means "land of the century plant." The century plant's sprouts look like bamboo. Some people call it a tree. The Mexicon century plant grows to a height of about thirty feet. The plant does not have reddish, pearlike fruit. The prickly pear or cactus apple is reddish and grows on a cactus which looks like a century plant.
7. Fusang people make thread and paper from Fusang trees.	Archeologists have found that Mexican Indians made thread from century plants, and a form of paper can also be made from them.
8. Fusang has no forts or armies.	Archeologists have found that around 400 A.D. the Mexican Indians were at peace.
9. Hwui Shan gave the emperor of China a mirror-like object from Fusang.	Archeologists have found that some Mexican Indians used mirrors made of polished stone.
10. Fusang has carts pulled by horses, cattle, and reindeer.	Archeologists have found that the Mexican Indians put wheels on their toys. There is no evidence as yet to show that Indian adults made use of the wheel. Spaniards brought the first horses and cattle to the Americas after 1500 A.D. The reindeer nearest to Mexico are found in Norway and Siberia. Hwui Shan probably stopped over in Siberia.

3. Hypothesizing activities can be built into a forced-choice value clarification procedure.[3] Have all your students gather in the center of the room. At one end of the room, write on the chalkboard the word *city;* at the other end of the room, write *country*. Then have the students move toward the word with which they more closely identify, pair off, and discuss their choices. The following are among the many additional word pairs you might use: grouper–loner, spender–saver, quiet–noisy, read a book–go to a party, Cadillac–Volkswagen.

4. Several hypothesizing possibilities exist. For example, while the students are still in the center of the room contemplating their choices, have them try to guess how one of their acquaintances will choose. After the choices are made, discuss with the class how accurate their hypotheses were.

5. After all choices between pairs have been made, ask the students to hypothesize about human behavior by matching words from several pairs. For example, a student might hypothesize that those who chose *country* also tended to choose *loner*. This hypothesis can be checked out immediately by having all those who choose *country* stand and remain standing if they also chose *loner*. Discuss the results in terms of support or lack of support for the stated hypothesis.

---

[3] Adapted from Sidney B. Simon, Leland W. Howe, and Howard Kirschenbaum, *Values Clarification* (New York: Hart Publishing, Inc., 1972), pp. 94–97.

3

characteristics of data and inferences

Succinctly, we can think of *inquiry* as working with and making inferences from data. Because data and inferences play central roles in inquiry, we have elected to devote an early chapter to their characteristics. This chapter culminates in the presentation of a model of inquiry, which in turn sets the topical stage for subsequent chapters and for your involvement in various operations of inquiry. Chapters 4 through 7 encourage you to be actively involved with various inquiry operations on the premise that your understanding of the presentations will thereby be facilitated; however, we recognize that a variety of "involvement modes" will best support and sustain your learning interests. Therefore, the nature of your involvement in Chapters 4 through 7 will vary.

The Nature of Data

The ultimate goal of any investigation is to extend the existing frontiers of knowledge.[1] To accomplish this goal, investigators pose researchable problems (Chapter 2) and seek to shed some light on those problems by gathering evidence (data) and making statements (inferences) from the evidence.

When an investigator analyzes a problem, he gathers and processes facts, numbers, statistics, records, and other verifiable information. In the context of a particular problem, such information is called *data*. In a sense, data are like pieces of a puzzle. They begin to make sense only when enough pieces are found and fitted together to form a whole picture. The "picture" which an investigator constructs might be one of an ancient civilization, the behavior of a particular group, the way in which certain people use and adapt to their environment, or the effects of a chemical compound on human cell tissue.

If we wanted to investigate a scientific problem concerning human behavior, and we decided to begin by listing the facts, numbers, statistics, and other verifiable information pertinent to that problem, we would be gathering which of the following? (Circle the appropriate letter.)

A. opinions
B. data
C. generalizations

The correct response is B; we would be gathering data.

If his study does not yield all the pieces of the puzzle, the investigator might venture educated guesses about the missing pieces. In this case, which of the following would be missing?

A. opinions

[1] We shall use *inquiry* and *investigation* interchangeably, and therefore as synonymous terms. Similarly, the terms *inquirer* and *investigator* will be used synonymously.

B. data

C. generalizations

The correct response is B; the investigator would be making educated guesses about his *missing data*. His guesses could constitute hypotheses for additional investigations.

We have been somewhat abstract so far in our discussion of data; now we shall be more specific. Look at this page of the book and check the statements which represent data about the page.

_____ A. The page has the number 27 on it.

_____ B. This page is more interesting than the preceding page.

_____ C. The page is made of paper.

_____ D. The page contains too many vague words.

A and C represent data because they contain factual, verifiable information, whereas B and D do not.

Applying Your Knowledge of Data

Suppose that we are archeologists, social scientists interested in cultures of the past. In a sense, the archeologist is a combination anthropologist and historian who is interested in how men in various cultures behaved. Like other social scientists, archeologists try to extend the frontiers of knowledge about man's behavior. Often, they do this by sifting through the remains of the past to discover and examine artifacts left by peoples of bygone eras. Artifacts are clues to people's beliefs, values, and interests.

Therefore, artifacts are sources of data for us as archeologists. Working at a site, we have discovered an artifact, an old coin, shown in Figure 3. The coin can become a source of data which we will use to reconstruct a partial picture of the society of which the coin is an artifact. To initiate

Figure 3   Views of a coin artifact

such a reconstruction, we might list factual, verifiable information about the coin. In doing this, we would be using the coin as a

A. source of data
B. source of opinions
C. source of conjecture

A is the correct answer; we would be using the coin as a source of data.

Now examine the following list, which is based on observation of the artifact. Check statements which represent coin data.

_____ A. There is a representation of a face on one side of the coin.
_____ B. The coin tells us that these were deeply religious people.
_____ C. The words "We Trust the Gods" are printed on the coin.
_____ D. On one side of the artifact is a drawing of leaves.
_____ E. These people worshiped leafy plants as gods.
_____ F. We can tell from the artifact that these were peace-loving people.
_____ G. The face on the coin is a representation of the nation's king.

Statements A, C, and D are examples of data. Statements B, E, F, and G *may* be factual, but without access to more data than the coin artifact provides, we would have to consider these statements inferential. Inferences are not data; they are statements based on data.

Moving from Data to Inferences

Why piece the picture together? If working with puzzles is your kind of activity, then viewing the completed picture and feeling a sense of accomplishment may be your payoff. However, inquirers must go further. Having completed the data puzzle, they intellectually scan the resulting picture and make statements about what they see. Their statements about the pieced-together data are called *inferences*. As you probably suspect, inferences must be related to the completed data puzzle.

For example, if we were to say, after examining the coin artifact, that this society probably mass-produced such an object, we would be making an _____ (fill in with a word).

Inference

Do you feel that the foregoing is an acceptable inference? Check one:

_____ acceptable inference
_____ not an acceptable inference

Well, maybe, and maybe not—it depends on whether we have supportive data for such a statement.

List some possible supportive coin data for such an inference:

1. _____

2. _____

Our supporting coin data for the inference might include observations that the lettering is uniform and the coin is perfectly round.

If we said that the people who lived in the society represented by the artifact were religious people, would we be (A) listing data or (B) making an inference?

(B) Making an inference

Does the inference that the people are religious have data support?

_____ Yes   _____ No

There isn't enough support in our data bank to warrant such an inference. Students may say that the statement "We Trust the Gods" is proof of a religious culture. However, the statement could also be a statement in an ideal sense, and not practiced in a real sense by the members of the society.

Use the space below to explain in your own words the difference between data and inferences.

_____

_____

_____

_____

Data are factual, verifiable information. Inferences are statements based on data.

It is important to keep in mind that inferences are supported by evidence. From the following statements, select those which you think are inferences based on data gathered from the artifact. Let *I* stand for inference.

_____ A. These people attended worship services for the gods several days a week.

_____ B. These people mass-produced artifacts such as this one.

_____ C. These people had a written language.

_____ D. These people lived in magnificent houses.

Statements B and C are inferences because the artifact contains some supporting data. Statements A and D lack data support.

If, as archeologists, our task is to reconstruct part of the past based on our examination of the artifact, we must be careful not to project our inferences too far beyond our:

A. wild guesses
B. data
C. opinions

B is the correct response. Data are used to support inferences.

To summarize, we examined an artifact as a source of data from which we made inferences. These inferences helped us in a very preliminary way to explain and understand a culture of the past. Data and inferences, then, are integral components of an inquiry process.

An Instructional Application

Can students discover ideas about man's behavior, as a social scientist might? (Indeed, students might well try the coin artifact lesson from this angle.) Let us further respond to this question by posing another problem which students might investigate. Suppose a group of students is investigating the distribution of certain goods and services in their city. Each student chooses one service offered in the city.

Let us watch as one student attempts to answer the inquiry question, "How is the spatial distribution of the laundromats in our community alike and different for the years 1950 and 1970?" With the problem in mind, the student's first task is to select the proper data sources to enable him to answer the question. In this case, a city map, a 1950 telephone directory with Yellow Pages, and a 1970 directory with Yellow Pages are appropriate data sources.

The chart below summarizes the student-inquirer's activity so far.

STATING THE PROBLEM ⟶ SELECTION OF DATA SOURCES

How is the spatial distribution of the laundromats in our community alike and/or different for the years 1950 and 1970?	city map 1950 Yellow Pages 1970 Yellow Pages

Using the Yellow Pages, the student is now ready to gather the data. The following lists are compiled:

1950 YELLOW PAGES

Comet Cleaners	710 Grant Street FE 2-6256
Golden Falcon Laundry	915 Grant Street FE 2-3110
Hudson Laundry	745 Flag Street TU 3-4848
Red's Cleaners	393 Flag Street TU 3-4620
White Way Cleaners	867 Adams Street TU 3-3106

1970 YELLOW PAGES

ABC Rainwash	375 Grant Street 332-5435
Comet Cleaners	710 Grant Street 332-6256
Golden Falcon Laundry	915 Grant Street 332-3110
Milky Way Cleaners	607 Grant Street 331-4000
Phil's Coin-O-Mat	680 Grant Street 331-6161
Speedy Wash	727 Fifth Avenue 332-5549
White Way Cleaners	867 Adams Street 883-3106

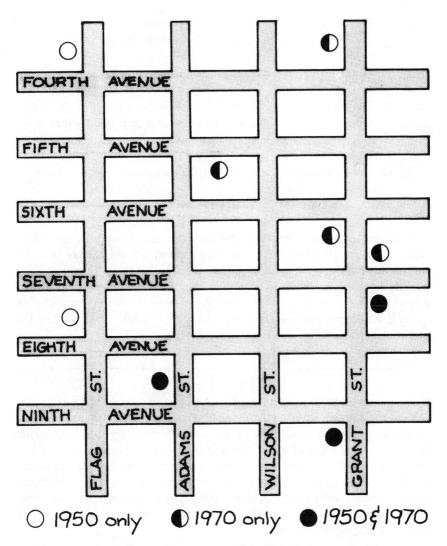

Figure 4 Distribution of laundromats: 1950, 1970 in Community X

After he plots the distribution of the laundromats on a map (see Figure 4), our inquirer can examine the spatial distribution of laundromats during the time periods under consideration. His inferences will have to do with speculation about the changes which have occurred. Look over the data that have been presented and decide which of the following inferences are justified. Check inferences which have data support.

_____ A. Poor locations forced two of the laundromats to close.

_____ B. An apparent need for more public clothes-washing facilities has developed.

_____ C. People in this community make a greater effort to keep clean than people in other towns.

_____ D. The newer laundromats are located near large apartment buildings.

_____ E. Some of the newer laundromats are located near one another.

_____ F. Larger numbers of people now use laundromats because the washing machines are newer than their own.

_____ G. There are more laundromats in 1970 than there were in 1950.

B is an appropriate inference because the laundromat increase data support it. Similarly, E and G have data support. A and D may be valid statements, but our investigation produced no data support for them. Such educated guesses could be used as hypotheses in initiating future investigations (Chapter 2). C and F are examples of guesses which have negligible utility for the present investigation, although F might be considered a potential hypothesis for a different investigation.

Let's now reexamine inference B: "An apparent need for more public clothes-washing facilities has developed." We labeled this inference as appropriate, given the conditions of our inquiry involving the laundromat data. What were some of of the needs that necessitated additional laundromats? How might the following kinds of data help answer this question: census data, the types of dwellings in the community, population densities, family incomes, age of surrounding structures? Later we will use such data as we elaborate on such operations of inquiry as gathering and processing data and making inferences.

A Model for Inquiry

Figure 5 represents the inquiry operations the student-inquirer followed in the laundromat investigation.

This inquiry model with its five operations—stating a problem and hypothesizing, selecting data sources, gathering data, processing data, and making inferences—will be used as a point of departure for subsequent chapters. Let us attempt to place it within a perspective which facilitates its employment.

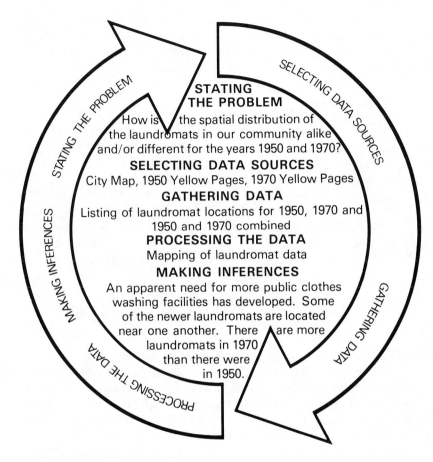

STATING THE PROBLEM

SELECTING DATA SOURCES

STATING THE PROBLEM
How is the spatial distribution of the laundromats in our community alike and/or different for the years 1950 and 1970?
SELECTING DATA SOURCES
City Map, 1950 Yellow Pages, 1970 Yellow Pages
GATHERING DATA
Listing of laundromat locations for 1950, 1970 and 1950 and 1970 combined
PROCESSING THE DATA
Mapping of laundromat data
MAKING INFERENCES
An apparent need for more public clothes washing facilities has developed. Some of the newer laundromats are located near one another. There are more laundromats in 1970 than there were in 1950.

MAKING INFERENCES

GATHERING DATA

PROCESSING THE DATA

Figure 5   A model of inquiry

In the investigation of the spatial distribution of laundromats for two different years, we described an orderly sequence of stating a problem and hypothesizing, determining data sources, gathering data, processing data, and making inferences. In practice, the path of the investigation is not always so direct. Even though an investigator may be involved primarily with a particular operation of inquiry (such as gathering data), he carries out that activity while looking through the lens of the other inquiry operations. For example, it would do little good to formulate an investigative problem if the data called for were inaccessible. Similarly, collecting data that are relevant to a problem can still result in an investigative disaster if the task of processing the data proves insurmountable.

Therefore, to the circular flow of activity shown in Figure 5, we can add a network of expressways, overpasses, and bypasses which link any two operations, or sets of operations, and thereby accommodate the "side trips" that become necessary for movement along the main routes. To treat the five operations of the model as immutably fixed and ordered is to violate the spirit in which they are presented.

Summary

Data may be thought of as factual, verifiable information. Data are found in various forms: for example, photographs, letters, documents, diaries, paintings, books, and artifacts. The point is that things become data when they are pertinent to the problem in question. Data form the substance of an investigation in the sense that they are what the inquirer selects, gathers, and processes. Having done this, the inquirer begins to say things about the data, which we have called inferences. Inferences are the result of the investigator's inductive leap from his data in order to reach conclusions and solutions of his stated problem.

Instructional Implications

In reading this chapter on the characteristics of data and the relationship between data and inferences in scientific investigation, you may have thought about the application of these ideas in your classroom. We want to note that we have used both the coin lesson and the laundromat lesson extensively with both teachers and students. We have found them rather purposeful lessons. Try them with your students. In addition to the two lessons developed in this chapter, the many others which follow will help you begin to implement an inquiry-centered classroom.

In this and several subsequent chapters, we have grouped the activity examples somewhat arbitrarily into two categories: those for *younger learners* and those for *older learners*. However, with minor modification most of the examples could be used with either group.

EXAMPLES FOR YOUNGER LEARNERS

1. To convey the idea of inference-making from data, explain that a simple picture puzzle with a number of pieces missing presents a situation somewhat analogous to the circumstances of the investigator who must use the data he has (the puzzle pieces present) to make inferences about missing data (the missing puzzle pieces). This situation is common in historical

inquiry. The children can put a puzzle together on a sheet of plain paper and sketch their "inferences" about how the incomplete portions of the puzzle look. Each investigator may draw the missing portion slightly differently, but in every case the inferences must reflect the data. When the children have presented their inferences, have the class discuss the notion that no one knows for sure what the missing area looked like, just as the historian cannot always "prove" that his reconstruction of past events is totally accurate.

2. Present your students with a dilemma-centered situation in human behavior. After you have read the following story, help the children fill out a chart similar to the one in Table 3. Then lead the students to see that the questions on the left side of the chart have definite answers (data), while those on the right side of the chart are answered in terms of inferences.

Mary checked a book out of the school library and took it home after school was out. She put it on a table at home and then ran out to play. Her brother, Tim, who was four years old, found the book and cut pages out of it with a pair of scissors. The book was ruined.

Table 3 A chart for analyzing a dilemma-centered situation

What people were in the story?	What happened?	How did it happen?	Who is responsible?	How could things have been different?

3. A useful tool for contrasting data and inferences in social science inquiry is the behavior specimen. Analogous to the laboratory specimens used in the natural sciences, the behavior specimen provides a glimpse of human behavior for students to analyze. The following script, which can be role-played or put on tape, presents a disagreement over bedtime between Diane and her grandmother.

Grandmother: Diane, it's 9:00 and time for you to go to bed.
Diane: Oh, gee, Grandma, my favorite program is coming on now.

Grandmother: Well, that's too bad. Anyway, you'd say that no matter what time it was.

Diane: No, I wouldn't! If Mom and Dad were here they'd let me stay up!

Grandmother: Well, they're not here, and I'm in charge tonight. So off to bed.

Diane: Please let me stay up for just a little while. Then I'll go to bed.

Grandmother: When your father was your age, he was in bed every night at 8:00. He'd come home from school, do his chores, eat his dinner, do his homework, and go to bed.

Diane: That's not the same thing. Things are sure different now that you're living with us. I wish you'd never come to stay here. Good night!

After the students have acted out or listened to the behavior specimen, ask them to record as many items of data *(what* happened?) as they can. Then have them build inferences and offer explanations from their data base.

4. Textbooks offer students a good opportunity to contrast statements of data with statements of inference. The following excerpt is from a typical intermediate-grade social studies textbook.

Mexico: Life in a Mexican Village

Village people work very hard for very little money. But they are cheerful and always ready to share what they have. They love their children and want big families, even if it means sacrifice and more work. Their life is hard, but they have love and religious faith. So they are usually happy, and life is good.[2]

When the students have examined the excerpt, ask them to classify the statements as either "data" or "inference." One or more students may want to send a letter to the textbook author(s), seeking information about the nature of the data base from which certain inferences were made. In writing their letter, the students may want to pose the following questions:

1. Did the author arrive at these conclusions by using primary sources? Direct observation? Survey?
2. Did the author reach these conclusions by using secondary sources? How reliable are they?
3. Are these village people all alike?

Data	Inference

5. Have the students read the following statements about the Pilgrims. Then ask them to research an answer to the question which follows the textbook excerpt. This will encourage them to cite an example from history and will underscore the necessity in inquiry of an adequate data base.

> In England, the Pilgrims were not allowed to worship as they pleased. When the Pilgrims came to America, one of the things they wanted was the freedom to worship as they wanted. When they settled in America, the Pilgrims worshipped their way, but they would not allow others living in their colony to worship in different ways.

Ask the students whether they think the Pilgrims should have allowed others living in the colony to worship as they pleased. Obviously, many students will say initially that freedom of worship should have been allowed. A larger data base may cause them to see the complexity of the problem. For example, there was very little precedent for religious freedom for them to draw on. Also, the Pilgrims felt that certain restrictions were necessary just to hold their colony together through the illness and starvation-ridden winter.

EXAMPLES FOR OLDER LEARNERS

1. The case study "Hunter-Gatherers" furnishes students with seventeen data statements. Working in small groups, the students are assigned the following tasks:

1. Identify the major problems facing the Hunter-Gatherers.
2. Pose solutions to those problems.

HUNTER-GATHERERS DATA SHEET [3]

1. There were cave people who lived a long time ago.

2. These cave people believed that it was important to remain in the cave where they were born and where their ancestors had lived.

3. This group of people was a nonroving group of people bound to living in their cave by religion and tradition.

4. The cave people lived near a well which was the source of their water supply.

5. The men hunted for almost all of their food.

6. Each year the hunters had to travel greater distances to kill animals for food with fewer and fewer results.

7. During the growing season women gathered some wild growing grain, seeds, nuts, fruits, and roots.

8. Women were able to store a small amount of the roots for winter use.

9. Women ground the small amount of grain into a flour to store in small amounts for winter consumption.

10. The small amount of wild plant food was able to feed the group for about two weeks during the wintertime.

11. Even though people died during the winter from starvation, the population increased.

12. The women noticed that some wild grain grew at the same place each year. This was in an elevated place where soil was washed down to small two-foot square parcels of land.

13. Other wild grain did not grow in the same place each year.

14. During some spring seasons, floods from rains destroyed all wild growing plants and drove the animals away.

15. When floods came, the winter was harsh because of poor grain growth, and starvation increased.

16. The year after a flood, there was more wild grain growing and it supplied winter needs for about three weeks.

17. One year the people built dikes to store water for wild grain to grow, and the yield was very good.

USING THE HUNTER-GATHERERS DATA SHEET

Source of Data: Hunter-Gatherers data sheet
Tasks: 1. Students will identify problems of the cave people.
                   2. Students will identify solutions to problems.
                   3. Students will supply inferences regarding possible aspects of culture change in the lives of the cave people.

[3] Written by Leo LaMontagne, Wellesley Curriculum Center, Wellesley, Massachusetts. Used with permission.

Procedure: 1. Tell the story of the Hunter-Gatherers to students.
2. Let students in small groups identify and discuss the problems of the Hunter-Gatherers.
3. After the groups have identified problems, try to identify alternative solutions to specific problems.
4. Allow for discussion time in which students may offer inferential explanations regarding culture change.

2. Use the aerial photograph on page 114 to help students see the relationship between data and inferences. Give the students the following assignments, to be completed either in small groups or as an entire class.

1. On paper, make note of anything you see in the photograph which could be listed as an item of data (for example, trees, roads, bridge, river, lake, house, farmland).
2. Using the data you have gathered, respond to the following questions. The answers will be inferences.
   a. What type of climate would be found in the area shown? (Use such data clues as vegetation.)
   b. How do people make their living here? (Note farmland, urban area.)
   c. Is this a small, medium, or large city? (How many blocks long is the waterfront?)
   d. If you could walk through the streets of the settled area, what language would you need to know to converse with people? (Grid pattern suggests the United States, therefore you would need to know English.)
   e. What uses might the river have?
   f. Specifically, where could this place be?

3. The purpose of this exercise is to use increasing amounts of data to substantiate a hypothesis.[4] Give each student a copy of Map I (Figure 6) and ask him to guess where he thinks a major city could logically be located in Country X and explain why he chose that particular location. Then, one at a time, hand out the next three maps (land forms, rainfall, vegetation), which furnish new data, to see whether the students wish to reassert their original guesses or to change them in the light of new data. When the students have made their final guesses, have them find Country X in an atlas and see whether their guesses were correct. (Country X is actually Peru.)

[4] In Chapter 4 we shall say more about the relationship between a hypothesis and an inference. In general, a hypothesis is an educated guess that has less data support than an inference and is therefore more tentative. Investigations are conducted to determine whether hypothses can be supported.

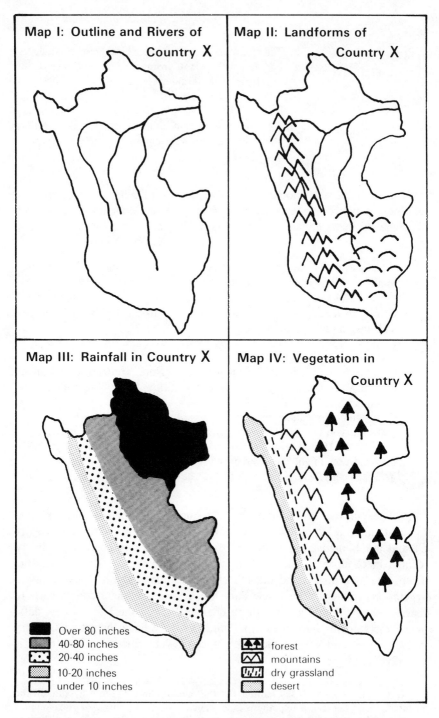

Figure 6 Four data source maps that can be used in making inferences about an unknown country

4

selecting data sources

The inquirer determines the most appropriate data sources for his investigative problem. A data source is any object, phenomenon, event, or person which can potentially give the investigator factual, verifiable information. The activities in this chapter will help you develop an intuitive feeling for the essence of this definition.

If you have read the preceding pages in this book, you have already worked with several data sources. For example, list the data sources which were used in the investigations in this list:

INVESTIGATIVE PROBLEM   DATA SOURCE(S)

What are the characteristics of   _____
the ancient society under investi-   _____
gation? (Refer to pages 27 to   _____
31.)

INVESTIGATIVE PROBLEM   DATA SOURCE(S)

How is the spatial distribution of
the laundromats in our commu-   _____
nity alike and/or different for the
years 1950 and 1970? (Refer to   _____
pages 32 to 34.)
                                     _____

Figure 7   Inquiry operation: selecting data sources

1. Coin artifact
2. 1950 telephone book Yellow Pages
   1970 telephone book Yellow Pages

Data sources are not elusive entities. Each of us is surrounded by potential data sources that are selectively activated when they are deemed appropriate to our investigative problem. For example, suppose an investigator is attempting to determine the characteristics of those who read books on inquiry. You have been selected as one of the subjects to be included in the investigation, but you are unable to meet with the investigator. However, you offer to make your wallet temporarily available for examination. How helpful have you been to the investigator?

Using your wallet and its contents (see Figure 8) as a data source, we can see possibilities for gathering data such as the following about you:

Your place of residence
Various personal characteristics such as age, weight, color of eyes, sex, marital status, occupation
The kinds of organizations you belong to
The extent of your education (university alumni card)
Where you shop (credit cards)
Your place of employment

To you, the wallet and its contents were probably useful only in that they gave you purchasing power, a means of identification, and the right to drive a car. However, the same contents proved to be a valuable data source, helping the investigator identify several of your characteristics.

A list of potential data sources is practically endless. Here are a few examples:

advertisements	magazines	newsreels
almanacs	newspapers	reference books
atlases	letters	diaries
artifacts	handbills	documents
census reports	video tapes	people
maps	study prints	directories
poems	filmstrips	pictures
films	slides	novels
textbooks	recordings	

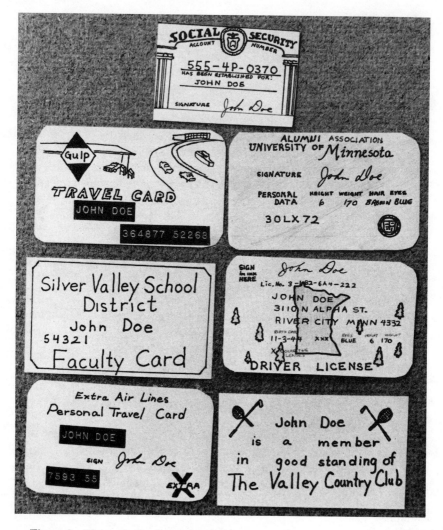

Figure 8 The contents of a wallet as data sources

Anything (bottle openers, trash mail, class notes) is a potential data source.

Characteristics of Data Sources

Let us now consider certain characteristics or attributes of data sources, in conjunction with the activity involving the wallet and its contents.

1. *A data source is essentially passive and dependent on an active inquirer.* The wallet and its contents were "activated" as a data source by the investigator in connection with his investigative problem. Before the investigator's action, the wallet and its contents served a different set of functions for your activities.

2. *A single data source rarely has the potential to supply an investigator with a complete pattern of relationships.* On the basis of the single data source we used (the wallet and its contents), are we ready to describe the characteristics of those who read books on inquiry? Do we have sufficient data even to describe adequately *your* characteristics? The answer to both questions is *no*. Among other things, additional data sources are required in this investigation.

3. *A data source is a means to an end in the process of inquiry.* The reason for examining the wallet and its contents was to collect data that would be processed to help the investigator make inferences about reader characteristics and behaviors.

MAKING AN APPLICATION

By now you should be ready to apply the above generalizations concerning the characteristics of data sources. Use your own words to explain briefly (two or three sentences) what each of the following three statements means, when applied to the coin artifact lesson (pages 27 to 31).

1. A data source (the coins in this instance) is essentially passive and dependent on an active inquirer.

_____

_____

_____

_____

2. A single data source rarely has the potential to supply an investigator with a complete pattern of relationships.

_____

_____

_____

_____

3. A data source is merely a means to an end in the inquiry process.

We answered as follows:

1. While the artifact is a *source* of data, it presents the investigator with no inferences or conclusions; he must develop them himself. In this way the artifact contrasts with descriptive accounts presented in textbooks, which often furnish the learner conclusions and ready-made inferences, thus rendering him passive.
2. While the artifact can help the investigator formulate some tentative ideas about a culture's technology and religious attitudes, he will have to examine additional data sources (perhaps he has also found a ball-point pen, a child's diary, a credit card, and a monkey wrench) before he can make more definitive statements about the patterns of that culture.
3. While the role of the artifact in the investigative process is a key one, it is also intermediate; the basic purpose of the inquiry in this instance is not to study coins, but to generate inferential knowledge about a culture.

Primary and Secondary Data Sources

Suppose you are investigating the cultural characteristics of the Hopi Indians. You are able to locate the data sources displayed in Figure 9, which are part of the program, "Project Social Studies—Minnesota." [1] In Figure 9, the data sources on the Hopi are divided into two groups. Stop reading for a moment and think of several criteria statements we might have used in making the division.

---

[1] Edith West, "The Family of Man: A Social Studies Program," *Hopi Indians* (Newton, Mass.: Selective Educational Equipment, Inc., 1971).

Figure 9   Two groups of data sources on the Hopi Indians

We have distinguished among the Hopi data sources according to (1) primary sources and (2) secondary sources. The data sources in group A are primary data sources because they are part of Hopi culture. The book on the Hopi has been processed for the learner, while the other data sources have not, and thus it is a secondary data source. Proximity to events and degree of processing are basic distinctions between primary and secondary data sources.

Similarly, we used your wallet and its contents as a source of data about your characteristics and behavior. Suppose that someone has written your biography, and therefore we have another data source at our disposal. In

this case, the wallet and its contents are a _____

data source and the biography is a _____ data source (primary, secondary). Ordinarily, an investigator selects primary data sources over secondary sources. His preference for primary sources is based on the assumption that secondary sources, because they have been processed, subject him to someone else's opinions. Primary sources tend to be more neutral in this regard.

Try to categorize the data sources in Table 4 as primary and secondary.

Table 4   An exercise in differentiating between primary and secondary sources

Data Source	Check one	
	Primary	Secondary
Advertisements		
Almanacs		
Artifacts		
Atlases		
Census reports		
Diaries		
Directories		
Documents		
Encyclopedias		
Lectures		
Magazine articles		
Paintings		
Poems		
Presentations		
Reports		
Textbooks		

PRIMARY DATA SOURCES

Advertisements
Almanacs
Artifacts
Atlases
Census reports
Diaries
Directories
Documents
Paintings
Poems

SECONDARY DATA SOURCES

Encyclopedias
Lectures
Magazine articles
Presentations
Reports
Textbooks

You may have found some of the items in the list difficult to classify. Let's examine the idea of "degree of processing" more thoroughly. Certainly poems and paintings are "processed" materials. but we can distinguish between them and material processed specifically for learners. A letter written by a Colonial militiaman becomes an artifact, and thus a primary data source, to a student investigating the American Revolution, while an expository description on the same topic found in an American history text provides the student with a secondary data source.

Consider for a moment our earlier example of how an investigator might inquire into the methods of teaching social studies that were used in the schools in the 1950s (refer to the Prologue). One way to approach the problem would be to read curriculum textbooks which review the teaching methods in use at that time. Another way would be to find social studies textbooks and teachers' lesson plans from the period. Yet another way would be to interview former teachers and students from the 1950s. An investigator would probably do all three.

In each case the investigator would be using data sources. A curriculum book represents a secondary data source, filled with processed data. The reader of the text is at least once removed from what actually happened in classrooms in the 1950s. Textbooks and lesson plans, teachers and students are primary data sources because they were part of the actual events (our first criterion is proximity to events) and because they are essentially unprocessed (our second criterion is degree of processing).

Appropriateness of Data Sources

Oceans of potential data sources surround us. Our task is to select those sources that are appropriate for our particular investigation. Of course, some data sources are always inappropriate, and appropriateness is often a matter of degree. Some sources are more helpful than others. In the interest of saving time and energy, it is crucial that we choose those sources which serve the investigation best. If we decide to inquire into settlement patterns in the Tennessee Valley, Captain Cook's journal of his explorations in the South Pacific would be an inappropriate data source. Historical accounts and land-use maps made at different time intervals would be more fruitful data sources.

THE BATTLE OF LEXINGTON

To pursue the point about appropriate data sources, suppose that you are an investigator whose task is to reconstruct to the best of your ability an objective account of the Battle of Lexington. This battle was a skirmish between British soldiers and Colonial militiamen on the eve of the American Revolution. Eventually your task will be to make inferences about the battle from the data you have gathered. At this stage of the investigation, however, you are merely considering the appropriateness of a number of potential data sources, listed below:

1. Letters written by participants in the Battle of Lexington
2. A National League baseball autographed by Johnny Bench
3. The report of John Parker of the Lexington Men

4. A rare photograph of the mad monk, Grigori Rasputin

5. A letter (about the Battle of Lexington) from Joseph Warren, a colonist, to the towns in Massachusetts

6. The diary of John Barker, a British soldier present at the Battle of Lexington

7. A photostatic copy of General U. S. Grant's orders for the siege of Vicksburg

8. A letter from General Thomas Gage leader of the British soldiers in New England, to Lord Barrington, British Secretary of War

9. The report of Major Pitcairn, leader of the British soldiers at Lexington, to General Gage

10. A textbook titled *Our Nation's Heritage*

11. A book titled *Great Voyages of Discovery*

Sort the potential data sources into two categories: (1) probably appropriate, and (2) probably inappropriate. Also, note whether each data source is primary (P) or secondary (S). Enter the number of the data source in the appropriate column.

PROBABLY APPROPRIATE	PROBABLY INAPPROPRIATE
1-P	

PROBABLY APPROPRIATE	PROBABLY INAPPROPRIATE
1-P	*2-P*
3-P	*4-P*
5-P	*7-P*
6-P	*11-S*
8-P	
9-P	
10-S	

Applying Your Knowledge

Here is part of one of the appropriate primary sources listed above—a letter written in Colonial America by a witness of the Battle of Lexington.

> . . . The British soldiers came to Lexington on their way to Concord. Seeing these soldiers, the men from Lexington ran in different ways. The British soldiers ran toward them and began firing. Eight of the Lexington men were killed and five or six were wounded. The British soldiers kept firing. Only those who weren't killed or wounded escaped. . . .[2]

Using this source, let us further refine the notion of the "appropriateness" of a data source. List some of the questions you, as an investigator, would pose as you further analyze the appropriateness of this data source in terms of the investigative problem of reconstructing the events of the Battle of Lexington. We have started you off. Try to list three additional questions.

1. _____

2. _____

   _____

   _____

3. _____

   _____

   _____

4. _____

   _____

   _____

Other questions might include:

What was the witness's purpose in writing the letter?
What was the role of the witness during the battle? A soldier on one of the sides? A local farmer? A newspaper reporter?

[2] We shall work more extensively with this letter, and others, in Chapter 7.

How long had the witness lived in Colonial America?

What personal interests did the witness have in the war? Potential business gains and losses? Relatives serving as soldiers? Immediate relatives still living in Britain?

How do the accounts of this witness compare to the observations of others at the battle?

What was the educational level of the witness?

How old was the witness at the time of his observations?

The questions listed above are only a few possibilities; you have probably included additional questions that are relevant.

Later we shall revisit and further use several of the data sources classified as appropriate for synthesizing the events of the Battle of Lexington.

AT THE FOOTBALL GAME

Suppose you are interested in dealing with the question, "What are the attitudes of the people in a particular city toward the professional football team located in that city?" You have decided to use as your data-gathering device a personal interview. You drive to the stadium on the afternoon of the game and interview people as they leave the men's restroom. After you have talked with fifty people, you watch the remainder of the game with one eye on the fans seated around you, to spot-check their attitudes. Then you return home and attempt to make inferences based on your data about the attitudes of the people of the city toward the local football team. How appropriate is your data source to your investigation?

_____ A. Very appropriate

_____ B. It's impossible to say

_____ C. Very inappropriate

We think the correct answer is C. Such a data source is very inappropriate. Your question concerns the attitudes of the people of the city toward the football team. What if some of the fans you interviewed were not city residents, but were in town merely to see the game? However, even if all your respondents were residents, it is uncertain that as fans they were any more representative of all the city's residents than the people in attendance at the Museum of Natural History, or those at the city zoo on that same day. Finally, there is no guarantee that the people coming out of the men's restroom are a representative sample of the people at the stadium on that day, or even a representative sample of a unique group that uses public restrooms at football games. Women fans, for example, would be automatically excluded. Your choice of an inappropriate data source would render your inferences invalid in regard to the question you posed. An investigator must seek a representative sampling of data sources, for the inferential statements he will make later in his investigation must be directly tied to his sources of data.

Summary

In this chapter, we have emphasized that inquiry tends to function best when the investigator is able to deal directly with data sources, and that potential sources of data are all around us. Further, we stressed that the basic passivity of primary data sources leads the learner to assume an active role. Having dealt systematically with data sources (especially primary sources), the learner may well begin to sense the inquiry potential of the many latent data sources in his environment which familiarity might otherwise have caused him to overlook.

Instructional Implications

1. Consider the following instructional situation: In Ms. Anderson's class, the students have been studying the Indian tribe which once inhabited the surrounding region. They have read accounts of the tribe in their textbooks, encyclopedias, and library reference books. In addition, groups of students have presented oral and written reports on various topics related to the activities of the tribe. The class has also seen and discussed a film about the Indians. On Wednesday, Ms. Anderson has a surprise for the class: she has borrowed a number of artifacts representative of the Indian tribe from a local museum and has arranged them on a table in the classroom. (Her display is similar to that in Figure 9). A card explaining its composition and function is placed beside each artifact. The students are excited about the display. Ms. Anderson tells the students that the display will remain in the classroom for two days and that they may examine the relics in their free time. She hints to the class that she may use the display as a test by removing the cards on Friday.

In this situation, although students and teacher were exposed to a group of artifacts, they failed to perceive them as data sources from which they could draw a number of inferences about the culture of the Indian tribe. The teacher missed an opportunity to involve the students as active investigators because her perception of learning was tied primarily to textbooks, encyclopedias, and films; she saw the artifacts only as a display or as possible sources of recall test items, rather than as sources of data relevant to an investigative problem. The "data sources" lacked instructional perspective and were treated as end-products. Unlike traditional descriptive sources of information—textbooks, encyclopedias, and films—these artifacts represented primary data sources from which students, acting as scientific investigators, might have posed questions, gathered and processed data, perceived relationships, and made inferences.

Unlike textbooks, primary data sources do not automatically supply conclusions to learners. This is a crucial point in the conduct of inquiry: the investigator must generate his own ideas in answer to problems or questions with which he has identified. The systematic analysis of situations, events, or problems becomes the student's responsibility, and the time-honored position of the textbook is preempted.

The teacher perceived the artifacts as ornaments rather than as data sources. The following questions might have presented the artifacts to the students as data sources:

How might you describe each artifact?

What relationships might exist between the artifact's structure and its possible use?

What are some other kinds of data that would lend support to your guesses regarding the functions of these artifacts?

What relationships in function might exist among the artifacts?

Using these artifacts, what description of this culture (inferences) can you make? How certain are you of your description?

What further questions do you have about the artifacts? (Resultant student questions might include the following: What is the origin of the artifacts? Are they unique, or common to the culture under study? Where would an archeologist expect to find these artifacts—in the dining room? the bedroom? the fields? a tool shed?)

Through his involvement with questions like these, the student moves from the passive role of viewing display items to an active role of seeking explanations about the culture which the artifacts represent.

2. It is frequently difficult to encourage students to question data

sources before accepting the inferences of others (or making their own). The following activity may be helpful if you face such a problem. As the teacher, you might say:

> Suppose that no one in this room lives in the United States. However, let us further suppose that during the past summer I visited the United States and brought back these objects: a set of Mickey Mouse ears from Disney-land, a post card picture of the Grand Canyon, a vial of water from the Mississippi River, and a small replica of the Statue of Liberty. Now, what is your opinion regarding the adequacy of these data sources in explaining the culture of the United States?

In responding to the question, the students can begin to differentiate be-tween the culture that is projected to the tourist, or any other "outsider," and the perceptions of those who are members of that culture.

3. To implement inquiry teaching, the teacher needs a wider spectrum of instructional material than a set of textbooks ordinarily offers. Potential data sources such as those listed near the beginning of this chapter must be translated into instructional materials relevant to programs of study and must be made readily available to classroom teachers.

Drawing from documents to write a section of history (Chapter 7), studying the Yellow Pages to determine business trends and land-use (Chapter 3), examining aerial photographs to study changes in man's use of land (Chapter 6), and gathering data from a coin artifact to piece to-gether the story of someone else's way of life (Chapter 3) are a few of the examples in this book which indicate an instructional need for a plentiful supply of both primary and secondary data source materials from which students can begin to inquire.

4. A different view of the inadequacies of teaching a subject such as history as a series of immutable conclusions, even when data sources are abundant, is offered by Frank Ryan:

> . . . consider the eye witnesses, film footage, and numerous camera shots available as evidence on the events surrounding the assassination of President John F. Kennedy. And yet, people are in sharp disagreement on the piecing together of the events surrounding the tragedy! One can readily see how those responsible for piecing together the events into a coherent discourse (i.e., historians) will write (and in fact already have written) *histories* versus *a single history* of the assassination. Contrast the available evidence for writ-ing histories of President Kennedy's assassination with the relative paucity of information surrounding important events in the Civil War. How ludicrous

to teach *the* causes for the Civil War and *the* attitudes of the colonists during the Revolutionary War.[3]

5. Even if the only set of materials in the classroom is a textbook series, the teacher can recast it as a data source, instead of an often unquestioned source of inferences. Presumably, textbooks, film strips, films, and the like are created from a data base, and that data base can be scrutinized, even in the elementary grades. For example, one of the newer social studies programs contains the following excerpt on Admiral Byrd:

> . . . The men were near the North Pole.
> All at once they heard a strange sound.
> Something was wrong with one motor.
> Should they turn back?
> Should they keep going?
> They were so near the North Pole.
> They wanted to go on.
> But they were far away from land.
> What if the airplane crashed?
> "We will try to get the motor started," said Byrd.
> "I think we can make it.
> We will try."
> Soon Byrd shouted,
> "We made it! We are over the North Pole!"
> Byrd and Bennett were happy.
> They were the first men to fly over the North Pole.[4]

The following questions could involve the students in an analysis of the data base for the Byrd excerpt: What are possible data sources that might lead to such "conclusions" as "They were the first men to fly over the North Pole"? What are possible data sources for the direct quotations that are used? Which of the sources we have mentioned are primary sources? In your opinion, did the author use the kinds of sources we have mentioned? What are your reasons for your opinions?

Students could even write to the authors to pose such questions. Unfortunately, many students are never taught to scrutinize the inquiry activities of others (commonly referred to as the "scholarliness" of a work). Instead,

[3] Frank L. Ryan, *Exemplars for the New Social Studies* (Englewood Cliffs, N.J.: Prentice-Hall, Inc., 1971), p. 73.

[4] Marie M. Richards, Coordinator, "Concepts and Inquiry: The Educational Research Council of American Social Science Program," *Admiral Byrd* (Boston, Mass.: Allyn & Bacon, Inc., 1970), pp. 21–23.

they are force-fed the end products of someone else's thinking. For example, suppose that a teacher has used the excerpt on Admiral Byrd's expedition as part of a social studies reading assignment, with the objective that the students be able to recall the content; thus, the students must receive the content unquestioningly. Small wonder that students might be confused when an article such as the one in Figure 10 [5] appears. Is the book account or the newspaper account "correct"? Certainly we do not have the answer. However, it is obvious that the two accounts reflect different data sources which have led to different versions of the same event. A healthy skepticism of the work of others and the tentative quality of interpretations of data are two of the scholarly attitudes we shall discuss in Chapter 8.

6. A spinoff from the idea of having students question data sources is to have them collect more than one data source on a present-day event. For example, do various newspapers cover a World Series, Super Bowl, or political convention differently in terms of the space they give to the event or in the ways they express points of view? What relationships, if any, exist between being the host city for such events and the types of newspaper coverage that are offered? How do the students' responses to such questions shape their use of the various newspaper reports as potential data sources for the events described?

7. Data sources are not necessarily hundreds of years old or from a culture other than our own. Each of us has used artifacts which are unknown to our students. For example, primary-grade students can begin to work with data sources as they offer hypotheses regarding the possible use of such "artifacts" as a fountain pen, a bottle of ink, and an ink blotter. Reprints of old catalogs [6] can be a source of other ideas. Some tools are unique to particular regions of the United States. For instance, students in Minnesota would have little difficulty recognizing a scraper tool used for removing ice from a car's windshield, or an elongated aluminum rake used for pulling snow off a house roof, but these same tools might be foreign to students in southern California and Florida.

8. Word artifacts can be studied. "Hang ten," "woodie," and "surf's up" might have meaning for a California surfer, but they sound like a foreign tongue to others. City dwellers may never hear "hackamore" and "stanchion" until they visit a farm. Similarly, spectators who are ignorant of such terms as "punt," "fly pattern," "split end," "fullback draw," and "pass option" may be totally confused at a football game.

[5] © 1971 by The New York Times Company. Reprinted by permission.

[6] For example, the *1902 Edition of the Sears Roebuck Catalogue* (New York: Bounty Books, 1969).

New York, N.Y. After years of smoldering controversy, it is now being argued openly, and hotly denied, that two of America's national heroes, Admirals Robert E. Peary and Richard E. Byrd, failed to reach their avowed goal, the North Pole.

The charge that Peary never reached the pole appeared earlier in the conservative United States Naval Institute Proceedings and is answered in the December issue by Peary's grandson, Edward Peary Stafford, a retired Navy commander.

The attempt to downgrade Byrd appears in a book published this year by Random House. Much of the book's contents were endorsed earlier this month by Bernt Balchen, Byrd's pilot on his flight across the Atlantic and to the South Pole.

Balchen, now a retired Air Force colonel, was in fact the source of much material in the book entitled "Oceans, Poles and Airmen." Its author was Richard Montague, formerly a foreign correspondent for the old New York Herald Tribune and foreign editor of Newsweek magazine.

Regarding both Peary and Byrd, the skeptics argue that, considering the circumstances, neither man could have made it to the North Pole and back in the elapsed time of each attempt.

Peary in 1909 traveled across the ice floes with four Eskimos and a black American, Matthew Henson. Byrd in 1926 flew from Spitsbergen, Norway, with Floyd Bennett as his pilot, while Roald Amundsen and his colleagues were there preparing for their flight to the pole in an airship.

Montague writes that Bennett, who died in 1928, later told Balchen that early in the flight an oil leak had developed and that Byrd had ordered a return to within sight of Spitsbergen. There, although the leak stopped, they allegedly flew back and forth for 14 hours before returning to their base and a hero's welcome.

Balchen also argued that, considering the capabilities of the plane, the distances, times and wind conditions involved, Byrd could not have reached the pole. His claim to have done so, Montague says, "seems to have been the biggest and most successful fraud in the history of polar exploration."

It is well known that there was ill feeling between Byrd and Balchen.

Some of the charges against Byrd were contained in a book by Balchen entitled "Come North With Me," published by E. P. Dutton & Co., Inc., in 1958. However, influential friends of the Byrd family brought such pressure to bear on Dutton that extensive passages were deleted or revised in later editions.

The charge against Peary was written by Dennis Rawlins, a writer and specialist in planetary motions. He said Peary's account of his navigation across the hundreds of miles of pack ice to the pole was "the sheerest navigational nonsense in one of its most crucial parts."

At no point, he said, did Peary take observations to determine his drift to one side or the other of his planned march due north, even though traversing ice floes in constant motion. Not, according to Peary's own account, until his alleged arrival in the vicinity of the pole did he take a series of sun sights to determine if he had drifted to the right or left of his course.

These observations, which Peary cited later to establish his claim, Rawlins said, could easily have been faked.

These elevations of the sun helped persuade a distinguished board of experts, convened by the National Geographic Society that Peary's claim was valid.

A similar board, convened by the same society, also confirmed Byrd's claim. However, the society was a sponsor of both expeditions.

Figure 10 One data source on Admiral Byrd's expedition

9. Younger as well as older students can assume the role of the archeologist as they grapple with the following problem:

Sometimes groups of people decide to place objects in a capsule and store it away for other people to open in later years. Let us, as a class, pretend that we are selecting objects for a time capsule which is to be opened one hundred years from now. Let us say that our time capsule is the size of the orange crate that I have brought in today. What are some objects we should consider placing in the time capsule? [7]

The objects the students suggest should be the data sources future archeologists might find most useful in describing our culture.

10. *Bibliographic notes.* Examples of programs that meet the need for data source materials include *MATCH*,[8] the *Holt Databank System*,[9] and the *Social Science Laboratory Units*,[10] at the primary level, and *Origins of Humanness—Patterns in Human History*,[11] *Social Studies Inquiry Program*,[12] *World History Through Inquiry*,[13] and *The High School Geography Project*,[14] at the secondary level. These programs stress the importance of direct student involvement in inquiry operations. Science programs which strongly emphasize student use of data sources include the *Elementary Science Study*[15] and the *Science Curriculum Improvement Study*,[16] at the elementary level, and the *Biological Sciences Curriculum*,[17] at the

[7] Ryan, *Exemplars for the New Social Studies,* p. 65.

[8] *The MATCH Project* (Boston, Mass.: American Science and Engineering, Inc., 1969).

[9] William R. Fielder, ed., *Holt Databank System* (New York: Holt, Rinehart and Winston, Inc., 1972).

[10] Ronald Lippitt, Robert Fox, and Lucille Schaible, *Social Science Laboratory Units* (Chicago: Science Research Associates, Inc., 1969).

[11] Malcolm Collier, *Origins of Humanness—Patterns in Human History* (New York: The Macmillan Company, 1969).

[12] John U. Michaelis and Robin McKeown, *Social Studies Inquiry Program,* "World Studies" and "Asian Studies" (Palo Alto, Calif.: Field Educational Publications, Inc., 1969).

[13] Byron G. Massialas and Jack Zevin, *World History Through Inquiry* (Chicago: Rand McNally & Co., 1970).

[14] Nicholas Helburn, *The High School Geography Project,* "Geography in An Urban Age" (New York: The Macmillan Company, 1969).

[15] Randolph Brown, Director, *Elementary Science Study* (New York: McGraw-Hill Book Company, 1968).

[16] Robert Karplus, Director, *Science Curriculum Improvement Study* (Chicago: Rand McNally & Co., 1968).

[17] William V. Mayer, Director, "Biological Science: Patterns and Processes," *Biological Sciences Curriculum Study* (New York: Holt, Rinehart and Winston, Inc., 1966).

secondary level. The *Minnesota Mathematics and Science Teaching Project* [18] is an outstanding example of how disciplines can be meaningfully brought together.

An exciting example of a program providing a source of data in the form of punched-out data cards, similar to those used in computer analyses, is Mitchell Lichtenberg's secondary social studies program, *Ward Twenty-three.*[19] Students retrieve information on the constituency of Ward Twenty-three, such as name, age, number of children, income, occupation, and grid location of property. Patterns of political, social, and economic behavior are also investigated.

---

[18] James H. Werntz, Jr., *Minnesota Mathematics and Science Teaching Project* (Minneapolis: University of Minnesota, 1970).

[19] Mitchell P. Lichtenberg, *Ward Twenty-three* (Shrewsbury, Mass.: Educational Systems Research, 1971).

5

gathering data

Scientists choose among a variety of procedures for collecting and recording data. We refer to procedures for collecting and recording data as *data gathering techniques,* and to the devices used to carry out the procedures as *data gathering tools.* Let's expand the definitions of these two terms and attempt a series of applications.

Eight Data Gathering Techniques

The specific procedures you choose for gathering data will vary with your investigative problem and the nature and availability of your data sources. For example, you may interview people to determine their feelings toward open and free schools, administer a questionnaire concerning the public's TV viewing habits, observe individual animal behavior within a baboon

Figure 11   Inquiry operation: gathering data

troop, or test the achievement of students in an inquiry and noninquiry learning environment.

Now, to see whether we are communicating effectively, list the procedures indicated in the last paragraph for collecting data; that is, list the four data gathering techniques we mentioned. We have supplied the first one for you.

interview, _____, _____, _____

Data gathering techniques: interview, questionnaire, observation, testing.

We shall consider a total of eight data gathering techniques: direct observation, participant observation, indirect observation, questionnaire, interview, testing, scaled measurement, and physical measurement.[1] A description of the type of investigative activity associated with each technique follows.[2]

In practice, your frame of reference will influence your use of each technique. For example, one might observe a basketball game as a sports writer for the local newspaper, as a scout for a rival team, or as the publicity man for the home team. The technique (observation) is the same in each instance, but the vantage point of the observer varies.

DIRECT OBSERVATION

The investigator who employs the technique of direct observation obtains data from first-hand experience—he personally sees, hears, smells, tastes, or feels. For example, to determine the kinds of questions teachers pose in the classroom, the investigator sits in on a class session and observes questioning activity.

PARTICIPANT OBSERVATION

Participant observation is a form of direct observation in which the perspective of the investigator is from the inside of the activity. The investigator actually enters into the event and becomes a part of it, as he is simultaneously directly observing it. Participant observation is particularly useful to anthropologists who study other cultures. For example, to learn of the characteristics of a tribal culture, the investigator would attempt to gain entrance to the tribe and then to make observations from the perspective

---

[1] The eight data gathering techniques listed can be subsumed under three general methods of data gathering: observation (direct, participant, indirect); questioning (questionnaire, interview); and measurement (testing, scaling, physical measurement). Other data gathering techniques included under the measurement method are: projective, inventory, and sociometric. See David J. Fox, *The Research Process in Education* (New York: Holt, Rinehart and Winston, Inc., 1969).

[2] You may find it helpful to refer concurrently to the examples of instructional applications given for each data gathering technique. See pages 72 to 78.

of a participant. We might say that the role player George Plimpton was a participant observer as he temporarily assumed the quarterbacking role for the Detroit Lions, in an attempt to determine the feelings, attitudes, and pressures of a professional football player.[3]

INDIRECT OBSERVATION

Using indirect observation, the investigator experiences an event vicariously—through an intermediary—rather than at first hand. Observations may be made indirectly by viewing a film or a TV transmission (live or recorded), by examining documents and notes made by a direct observer, or by examining artifacts separated from their original locale.

The indirect observer's view of an event is more restricted than the direct observer's, and his use of his five senses can be sharply curtailed. For example, someone who attends a football game (direct observation) can look at the game, the players' benches, members of the crowd, or the sky, at will. However, someone who watches the game on TV (indirect observation) is restricted to the camera's view (the cameraman can be thought of as the direct observer). The TV observer, unlike the actual game viewer, is restricted to the use of two senses for observing the game— sight and hearing. A telecast is an indirect experience; simply because the viewer sees only what the cameraman allows him to see and is subjected to the commentator's point of view.

QUESTIONNAIRE

The use of a questionnaire in inquiry means that the kinds of data to be considered are selected and ordered by the investigator before the event occurs. Questions are submitted, and responses are entered on paper.

INTERVIEW

In an interview, the investigator questions his respondent and uses personal interaction in collecting data. An example of a totally structured interview is the poll.

TESTING

In testing, a problem is posed for the respondent and his response is evaluated by some value criterion such as "right–wrong," "well done–

[3] George Plimpton, *The Paper Lion* (New York: Harper & Row, Publishers, 1966).

poorly done," "creative–stereotyped." [4] Tests may be verbal (questions administered verbally, answer written or spoken), or nonverbal (performance tests).

SCALING

When he uses the scaling technique, the investigator has the respondent order a set of concepts or items along a criterion continuum. For example, he might ask students to mark how important various school activities are to them, using the scale shown in Table 5.

Table 5   Rating Scale

	Rating				
Activity	*No importance*	*Slight importance*	*Moderate importance*	*Very important*	*One of most important activities*
Attending school athletic contests					
Attending school assemblies					
Holding a school job, such as cafeteria worker					

PHYSICAL MEASUREMENT

The investigator can also assess such physical characteristics as height, weight, circumference, intensity, and acuity (visual or auditory) of the animate and/or inanimate. For example, when you step on a bathroom scale or note the amount of gasoline needed to fill your car's gas tank, you are using the physical measurement technique.

We offer specific classroom applications for each of the data gathering techniques in the Instructional Implications section of this chapter. They should help you distinguish further between the eight classifications of data gathering techniques.

---

[4] Fox, *The Research Process in Education*, p. 584.

Basic Data Gathering Tools

Data gathering tools are necessary to implement any data gathering technique. For example, to record the data from an interview, the investigator might use a pencil and paper or a tape recorder. We will refer to pencils, paper, and tape recorders as examples of potential *basic tools* for data gathering. A data gathering tool is, therefore, any device which facilitates the implementation of a data gathering technique. Tools help the investigator operationalize the data gathering technique. Examples of basic data gathering tools follow.

BASIC TOOLS FOR IMPLEMENTING A DATA-GATHERING TECHNIQUE

Recording tools:	Tape recorder, paper, pencil (for listing, tallying, noting, plotting)
Observing tools:	The senses: eyes, ears, nose, tongue, hands; cameras: TV, movie, still, videotape
Excavating tools:	For physical objects: hands, shovels, picks, and so on; for written objects: copying machines
Measuring tools:	Balance, scales, ruler, yardstick

Specialized Data Gathering Tools

In addition to his basic tools, the investigator often needs more specialized inquiry tools for carrying out various data gathering techniques. For example, to assess how well students are learning from a new instructional program, an investigator might develop a multiple-choice achievement test which would enable him to collect the relevant data. Similarly, to facilitate and systematize direct observation, especially where several observers are involved, the investigator might employ an observation guide, as in the example of the students observing kindergarten behavior (page 78). In addition to testing instruments and observation guides, other specialized tools used by investigators to implement data gathering techniques include interview guides, rating scales, rank-order scales, questionnaires, and computer applications. Table 6 summarizes the data gathering techniques and tools we have mentioned so far.

It is best to think of the various data gathering techniques and data gathering tools (basic and specialized) as potentially supportive of one another, rather than as mutually exclusive entities. For example, suppose a geographer were investigating a problem that necessitated going to a

Table 6 Examples of data gathering techniques and tools

Data Gathering Technique	Data Gathering Tools (Specialized)	Data Gathering Tools (Basic)
Direct observation	Various kinds of testing	Tape recorder
Participant observation	instruments, such as	Paper
Indirect observation	multiple-choice, essay,	Pencil
Questioning	true–false	Eyes
Interviewing	Observation guide	Ears
Testing	Interview guide	Nose
Scaling	Rating scale	Tongue
Physical measurement	Rank-order scale	Hands
	Questionnaire	Shovel
	Telescope, microscope	Pick
		Copying machine
		Balance
		Scales
		Ruler
		Yardstick
		Camera

neighborhood to conduct a field study. He could employ such data gathering techniques as questioning, interviewing, and observing, and consequently such basic data gathering tools as pencils, paper, tape recorder, camera, and the five senses, as well as such specialized devices as interview schedules and observation guides. He would consider the characteristics of the investigation, such as the investigative problem and the feasibility of gathering data from available sources, in determining which specific data gathering techniques and tools to use.

A Review

Let us now take time for a review. In the space provided, define the following terms in your own words and give one example for each term.

Data gathering technique: _____

_____

Example: _____

_____

Data gathering tool: _____

_____

Example: _____

_____

A data gathering technique is a procedure for gathering and recording data. A data gathering tool is any device used to carry out data gathering techniques. For examples, refer to Table 6.

Now that you have tested some of your recall knowledge, try to make several applications of your understandings. Place yourself in the position of an investigator who is interested in determining the new car preferences of people living in Lake City.

Hypothesis 1: Single people between the ages of eighteen and twenty-five prefer small, economical, foreign cars.

Hypothesis 2: Married people between the ages of eighteen and twenty-five prefer passenger cars and station wagons.

List below the data sources you would consider potentially useful for this investigation. You may refer to other parts of this book if you like.

_____

_____

Data sources might include documents, advertising, annual reports, sales records, people.

Now suppose that you conduct a search for relevant documents, annual reports, sales records, and advertising and are unable to come up with usable data. Therefore, you choose *people* as a data source. Having chosen a data source, what subproblem of this investigation do you now face? (Circle the appropriate letter.)

A. Collecting the data
B. Revising the study's problem in light of the data source you have selected
C. Making inferences on the basis of the results of your search for data sources

---

The main problem of the study provides the framework for the investigative decisions you must make; it requires no revision for this study. Also, it is too early for any inferring activity, because inferences are made from data and you haven't collected any yet. So, you could now begin to consider your procedures for collecting the data; that is, you could select the required _____ (data gathering techniques, topics of discussion).

Data gathering techniques. (If you answered this item incorrectly, please refer to earlier sections of this chapter for a quick review.)

Given *people* as your data source, list several data gathering techniques you might use to collect data on new car preferences. (You may refer to other parts of the chapter.)

We listed questioning, interviewing, and possibly observing (direct, participant, and indirect). Are our answers fairly similar to yours?

In using the data gathering techniques listed in the preceding frame, what are some classroom materials and equipment (that is, basic data gathering tools) that you might find useful? Try to respond without referring to other pages of the book.

Responses will vary with people's perceptions of what is (or should be) available in a classroom. However, we can probably all agree on such data gathering tools as pencils, paper, and tape recorders. More specialized data gathering tools that could prove useful include questionnaires, rating scales, interview guides, observation guides.

We shall pursue the new car preferences investigation no farther at this time. We hope you have noticed that the inquiry operations you were involved in while applying your knowledge can also serve as a strategical outline for instructionally initiating the new car investigation with your students. The inquiry operations were:

1. Identification of a problem, and statement of hypotheses
2. Selection of a data source
3. Use of techniques and tools to gather data.

Instructional Applications of Data Gathering Techniques

You may be wondering how data gathering techniques translate into instructional practice. We shall describe in the following pages specific instructional applications for the eight data gathering techniques we have introduced.

DIRECT OBSERVATION

1. Later in this chapter we describe a lesson in which students visit a classroom to observe the activity of kindergarteners during segments of the day. The observation guide (specialized tool of data gathering) on page 78 is used to facilitate carrying out this data gathering technique.

2. In a simulation game called DIG,[5] student teams plan and create a "culture," then construct artifacts representative of that culture. The artifacts (data sources) are then "planted." Other teams of student archeologists then go to the field (direct observation) to unearth the artifacts (using "basic" excavating tools) and then re-create the story of the culture, based on the gathered data.

[5] Contact Interact, P.O. Box 262, Lakeside, California 92040.

3. Frank Ryan describes a field study that students could conduct:

. . . a group of students might be asked to walk through a particular part of their neighborhood and write down their observations. A student might, for example, note a freeway and the position and types of structure near the freeway, such as service stations and motels on one side and various types of factories on the other. The purpose of plotting and noting characteristics of observed phenomena is to attempt to relate the observed phenomena. For example, what are possible reasons for a cluster of service stations in one area, or a group of warehouses near a particular intersection? Why do some homes have two-car garages, but in another neighborhood there are single-car garages or no garages at all? How have various buildings and sites been utilized in different ways over a period of time? (Geographers call this "sequent occupance.") How can these different utilizations be related to other phenomena in the surrounding area? [6]

PARTICIPANT OBSERVATION

1. Ask students to observe the behavior occurring around them as they participate in such activities as playing four-square, eating in the cafeteria, riding the school bus, or eating meals with their families. As he observes a family meal, the participant observer might decide to collect data which would answer these questions: Who is present at the meal? Do people sit in certain places? How is the food served? What do the people talk about? What rules are apparent? What roles do individual family members assume?

INDIRECT OBSERVATION

1. As part of the elementary program, "Man: A Course of Study," students examine the field notes of anthropologist Irven DeVore, who observed the behavior of baboon troops in East Africa. The students can "observe" a segment of baboon behavior through the field notes. Then the student-inquirers draw on their observations to suggest inferences concerning the behavior of the baboons and the purpose of the "observed" activity. The following excerpt could serve as a data source for such an experience.

June 28
    Mdomo is the animal who always jumps on the hood of a car first when it pulls up. But if the visitors begin giving him food, he is almost immediately

[6] Frank L. Ryan, *Exemplars for the New Social Studies* (Englewood Cliffs, N.J.: Prentice-Hall, Inc., 1971), p. 42.

displaced by Dano and Pua, who sit on each fender and reach around for more food. I threatened Mdomo away just now. When I do this, he then often threatens or chases another baboon. Dano and Pua are feeding side by side as usual. Dano barely dominant over Pua in feeding. The strange thing is that Dano and Pua seem to try *not* to show dominance over each other. They simply feed quietly side by side, and they will not show dominance unless I force them (with food, etc.). So although Dano is dominant, the two males are more relaxed than any two males I ever saw.

I threw a banana between Kovu's outstretched arms as he sat; he looked away from the banana, while Dano reached for the banana and took it. Dano is also dominant over Mark. So Dano/Kovu; Dano/Mark.[7]

2. One of the first-grade units of study from "Project Social Studies—Minnesota" [8] includes a series of Hopi artifacts to be used as data sources by student-"observers" (see Figure 9). Similarly, one of the MATCH [9] programs, "A House of Ancient Greece," includes a series of excellent replications of actual artifacts excavated from the Villa of Good Fortune in the ancient Greek city, Olynthus. Students take the role of archeologist-observers as they examine and attempt to determine the uses of the various artifacts.

3. In a secondary program, *From Subject to Citizen,*[10] students examine documents, pictures, historical accounts, letters, and lawyers' briefs as they compare English and American legal systems in regard to the key political science concept of "power." Another secondary program, the *High School Geography Project,*[11] has students observe a city by using such data sources as demographic charts, graphs, and maps, as they draw inferences for the purpose of building a simulated city.

QUESTIONNAIRE

1. Questionnaire lessons described in this book include "What time do you go to bed?" (Chapter 6), adapted from the first-grade guide for the pro-

---

[7] From "Selections from Field Notes, 1959, March–August," in Peter B. Dow, Director, *Man: A Course of Study* (Washington, D.C.: Curriculum Development Associates, 1970), p. 38.

[8] Edith West, *The Family of Man: A Social Studies Program,* "Hopi Indians" (Newton, Mass.: Selective Educational Equipment, Inc., 1971).

[9] *The MATCH Project* (Boston, Mass.: American Engineering, Inc., 1969).

[10] Nona Lyons, Director, *From Subject to Citizen* (Chicago: Denoyer-Geppert, 1970).

[11] Nicholas Helburn, *The High School Geography Project,* "Geography in an Urban Age" (New York: The Macmillan Company, 1969).

gram, *The Social Sciences: Concepts and Values;* [12] "What are the new car preferences of people in one town?" (Chapter 5); and "What is your favorite TV program?" (Chapter 6).

2. In the secondary program, *Sociological Resources for the Social Studies,*[13] students complete a questionnaire concerning their activities and attitudes. Student responses to the questionnaire are then used as a powerful springboard for discussing and analyzing the conditions and characteristics of poverty.

INTERVIEW

1. A highly structured interview is called a *poll.* Students at any level could poll other students at their school to sample how people might vote in an upcoming student council election, or how students feel about various activities and procedures at school, such as staggered lunchtimes, a free-choice period each Friday afternoon, and sixth graders working with fourth and fifth graders during social studies and science instruction.

2. Lesson 6 of the *Social Science Laboratory Units* [14] is entitled "How Do Social Scientists Conduct Interviews?" The lesson includes interviewing "do's" and "don'ts" and provides for an analysis of the recorded behavior of three students interviewing three other students with varying degrees of success.

TESTING

Surprisingly, newer instructional materials rarely provide opportunities for students to create and administer testing instruments, even though all students have repeatedly been on the "receiving end" of this data gathering technique. However, several applications that are easy to implement are described below.

1. Members of a class are randomly assigned to one of two groups, A and B. The two groups study a spelling word list using different methods. For example, group A students might practice by writing each word twenty-five times. Group B students could listen to a recorded voice describing common mistakes students have previously made in spelling each

---

[12] Paul Brandwein, et al., *The Social Sciences: Concepts and Values* (New York: Harcourt Brace Jovanovich, Inc., 1970).

[13] Robert C. Angell, *Sociological Resources for the Social Studies* (Boston: Allyn & Bacon, Inc., 1969).

[14] Ronald Lippitt, Robert Fox, and Lucille Schaible, *Social Science Laboratory Units, Teacher's Guide* (Chicago: Science Research Associates, Inc., 1969), p. 28.

word, and offering hints on how to memorize the correct spellings. The test, of course, is an administration of the spelling list to both groups, preferably at the same time.

2. Students in a physical education class may be interested in comparing the effectiveness of two methods of increasing the number of pull-ups they can do. Students are randomly assigned to two groups and pretested on their capability for doing pull-ups. For the next three weeks, students in group A devote fifteen minutes of each physical education period to practicing pull-ups. Students in group B use the identical fifteen-minute segment of each physical education period to run wind sprints. After three weeks, all students are post-tested on the number of pull-ups they can do. Pre- to post-test gain scores are compared between the two groups.

SCALING

1. On page 75 we described interviewing activity included in the *Social Science Laboratory Units*. After listening to the recorded interviews, the students mark on a scale their evaluations of how well the interviewing sessions were conducted. Four main questions are posed: How well did the interviewer explain the purpose of the interview? Did the interviewer try to make the person being interviewed feel relaxed and comfortable? How well did the interviewer succeed in eliciting meaningful answers to his questions? Did the interviewer succeed in keeping his personal opinions out of the interview? The students use three scales similar to the one below, one for each of the three interviews, as they respond to each of the four questions. Students are instructed on the meaning of each of the numbered loci (for example, 1 = very poorly done; 5 = extremely well done).

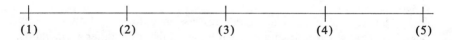

(1)   (2)   (3)   (4)   (5)

2. In another lesson in the *Social Science Laboratory Units*,[15] students rank-order their preferences among five activities: listening to records, swimming, reading mystery stories, reading adventure stories, and watching television. The results are processed and compared between male and female respondents.

---

[15] Ibid., pp. 35–42.

PHYSICAL MEASUREMENT

1. In the "Bulbs and Batteries" unit of the *ESS* science program,[16] students experiment with various possibilities for connecting batteries to supply current for light bulbs. The investigators then construct a meter (data gathering tool) to measure the light intensity that results from each set of connections.

2. First-grade students using the program, *The Social Sciences: Concepts and Values,*[17] collect data on the height and weight of class members as a prelude to considering similarities and differences and predicting future growth patterns.

• Students in the first few grades can begin to work as scientific investigators. We base this contention on our teaching experience, as well as on the experience of other teachers who have used the examples presented in this book. A simple questionnaire (containing only one question) can be especially workable with primary-age students. The following questionnaire lessons described in Chapter 6 are examples: "What time do you go to bed?" "What is your favorite TV program?"

Experiences with questionnaires provide the primary-age student with the necessary foundation for a fluid transition into the highly structured interview, which can take the form of a poll. Thus, students can verbally pose a single question, and later multiple questions, to a sample of people, for the purpose of collecting data.

We have had success with students at the intermediate grade levels in implementing various forms of observational techniques and employing specialized data gathering tools. For example, students might observe how kindergarteners spend their recess time. To facilitate this direct observation technique for gathering data, an observation guide (specialized data gathering tool) similar to the one in Table 7 could be used.

As students progress through instructional sequences, they can use increasingly sophisticated data gathering techniques and data gathering tools. For example, the single-question questionnaire can be expanded to include a series of questions which students have composed within a framework of validity and reliability considerations.

Along with the students' increasingly sophisticated use of data gathering techniques and tools, there is a corresponding decrease in the amount of

---

[16] Randolph Brown, Director, *Elementary Science Study, Teacher's Guide for Batteries and Bulbs* (New York: McGraw-Hill Book Company, 1968).

[17] Brandwein, et al., *Social Sciences: Concepts and Values, Teacher's Guide—Level One*, pp. 10–11.

Table 7   Observation guide for investigating kindergarten subculture

Name of Child Observed	Age or Grade of Subject	Date	Time of Day	Length of Observa- tion	Activities in Which Child Was Engaged
James	Kindergarten	Nov. 4	9.30–9:40 A.M.	10 minutes	Monkey bars Running Playing like horse
Anne	Kindergarten	Nov. 4	9:40–9.50 A.M.	10 minutes	Running Talking Monkey bars

teacher guidance given to the student-investigator. Many secondary-age students are fully capable of carrying out independent research that warrants publication.

Summary

Specific techniques are available for gathering data from data sources. We have introduced and suggested instructional applications for eight data gathering techniques: observation (direct, participant, indirect); questioning; interviewing; testing; scaling; and physical measurement. The implementation of a data gathering technique requires various tools of investigation, both basic and specialized.

6

processing data

We have developed several notions about data and inferences as basic considerations of any inquiry. We have also discussed and illustrated the following operations of inquiry: stating the investigative problem, selecting data sources, and gathering data.

Recall that the primary purpose of conducting an investigation is (check one):

_____ a. work with various data gathering devices.

_____ b. gather data.

_____ c. decide something from the data (that is, make inferences).

Deciding something from our data (c) is the correct response. The other two activities are among those we do to set the stage for making inferences.

Figure 12 Inquiry operation: processing the data

This chapter will develop the notion that the investigator must ordinarily process raw data in some way before he can draw inferences from those data. We shall consider various processing forms. Figure 13 illustrates several methods investigators use to process data.

The Need to Process Data

Suppose that student-investigators are trying to determine what behavior patterns exist, if any, concerning the time students go to bed each night.

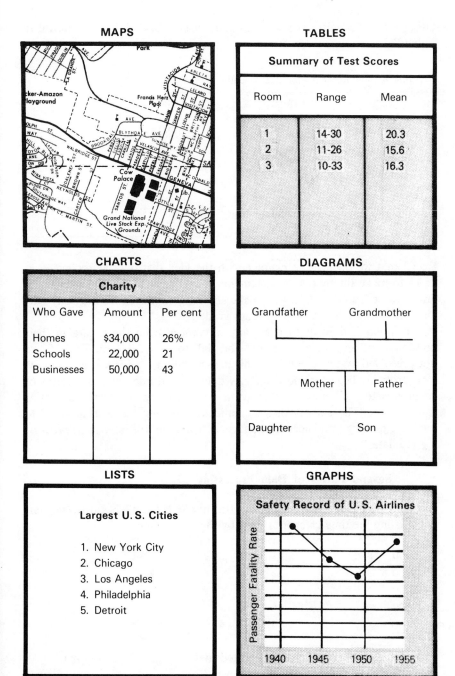

Figure 13   Six methods of data processing

Using a questionnaire, one seventh-grade class collected the data shown in Table 8.

Table 8   Bedtime data for one seventh-grade class

8:00	10:00
9:00	9:00
9:00	12:00
11:00	9:00
10:00	10:00
9:00	10:00
11:00	11:00
8:00	10:00
9:00	11:00
10:00	10:00
10:00	

Recall that we opened the chapter with the idea that data are collected in order to make inferences, or statements about the data. Now glance at the time data in Table 8 and try to make some inferences concerning any patterns of bedtime behavior of seventh graders.

We found it difficult to draw any inferences from these data in their present form, and we assume that you did, too. The data in Table 8 are not presented systematically. In this sense, they are unprocessed, or raw. You probably began to move the raw data around into various patterns or subgroups to facilitate the inference-making activity you were attempting to carry out. The activity of systematically "moving the data around" to facilitate making inferences is one facet of what we will refer to as *processing* the data.

Several Forms of Data Processing

What are some ways to process the bedtime data? Let's begin by sequentially listing the time categories used by the respondents:

8:00
9:00
10:00
11:00
12:00

Now, for each piece of data reported in Table 8, enter a tally mark (/) opposite the appropriate category above.

You have just been involved in processing data, and your results should resemble the following:

8:00	//
9:00	⫽⫽⫽ /
10:00	⫽⫽⫽ ///
11:00	⫽⫽⫽
12:00	/

The particular form an investigator chooses for processing his data depends not only on the problem he is investigating (which in turn shapes the kinds of inferences that will eventually be made), but also on the sophistication level of the audience for whom his research is intended. Therefore, we could also have translated the unprocessed time data into the form of a *line graph,* as shown in Figure 14. A variable form of the line graph is the *histogram,* such as the one in Figure 15.

We have used three processing forms with the time data: categorical listing, line graph, and histogram. Each of the three forms can help the investigator detect patterns and relationships in the collected data. Having processed the data, the investigator is now able to see for himself, and to present clearly to his audience, statements (based on the data) concerning such topics as the range of bedtimes (8:00 to 12:00) and the most popular bedtimes (9:00 and 10:00). Such data statements become the basic ingredients of inferences, a topic we shall develop in the next chapter.

We shall present several other methods for processing data in this chapter, and we shall employ further the forms of processing we have already introduced.

Time Out—To Pull the Inquiry Sequence Together

The operations of an inquiry sequence necessarily interrelate and affect one another. Thus, the operation of data gathering takes place in relationship to the investigative problem and the availability and accessibility of various data sources. Similarly, data are processed in accordance with the investigative problem, the type of data gathered, and the kinds of inferences the investigator wants to make. Our strategy in this book has been to focus on a specific operation of inquiry, but always within the context of its relatedness to the other operations. However, let us temporarily change this

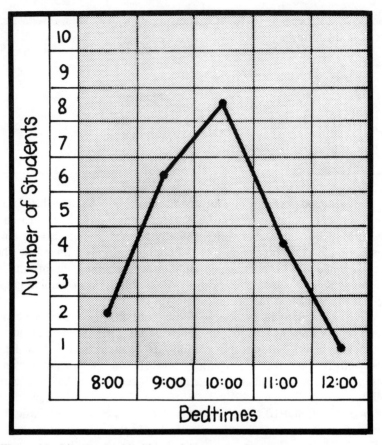

Figure 14   Line graph of bedtimes of one group of students

strategy. We shall concentrate on one investigative problem and consider several operations of inquiry that are implemented in solving it. We hope that this will help you see that inquiry is a series of interrelated operations, rather than a collection of disparate activities.

AN EXAMPLE OF INQUIRY

The Pan-American Coffee Bureau was interested in determining the coffee drinking habits of various age groups of people in the United States. The Bureau investigated several aspects of this overall problem, including how much coffee was being consumed daily on an individual basis. Examine the chart in Figure 16. It shows the average number of cups of coffee consumed

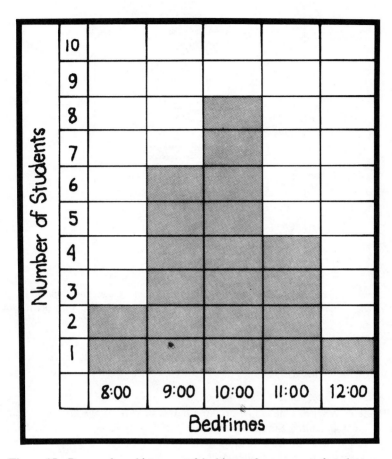

Figure 15   Bar graph or histogram of bedtimes of one group of students

per day by persons in various age groups in the United States during the winter of 1969. This chart is an example of *processed data*. The step in the inquiry process known as *data processing* follows the collecting of data and precedes the making of inferences.

To collect the data necessary to answer the question of daily per-person consumption of coffee by age groups, the Bureau interviewed a representative sample of six thousand Americans ten years and older during January and February, 1969. In each case the interviewer asked the respondent to recall the number of cups of coffee he drank during the day before the interview. In addition, data such as the respondent's age and other beverages he had consumed were collected. The people who were interviewed represent the data source.

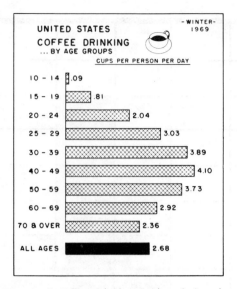

Figure 16 Histogram of coffee drinking habits of Americans (*Annual Coffee Statistics,* Pan-American Coffee Bureau, New York, 1968. Used with permission.)

To recount briefly the steps in the investigative process, let us examine the following synopsis:

1. *Problem:* What are the coffee drinking habits of various age groups of people in the United States? (To collect the data reflected in Figure 16, the following question was posed: How much coffee do people of various age groups in the United States consume per day?)

2. *Data source:* A representative sample of six thousand persons, ages ten to seventy, living in the United States. In this instance the investigator used a primary data source.

3. *Data gathering technique:* A personal interview was conducted in which respondents were asked to state the number of cups of coffee they could recall having drunk the day before the interview, the types and amounts of other beverages consumed on the preceding day, and their age. The resultant data included the number of cups of coffee drunk, types and amounts of other beverages consumed, and ages of respondents.

4. *Data processing:* A histogram showing the amount of coffee consumed by people in various groups, as well as a total for all age groups, was constructed (Figure 16). In this instance, the data regarding the types and amounts of other beverages consumed were not processed.

5. *Making inferences:* This topic is explored in the next chapter.

Data Processing as an Activity for Younger Investigators

You probably accept the idea that older students can gather and process data. But what about children of primary age? Can they become scientists who investigate problems systematically? Before you answer these questions with any degree of finality, locate a six- or seven-year-old and involve him in the following investigation. (Note: As we did in the preceding description of an investigation involving coffee consumpton, we are placing the data processing activity into the context of a sequence of inquiry activity. After you have read through this sequence of inquiry, you will be asked to identify the investigative activity that was occurring for each of the operations of the inquiry model which was presented in Chapter 3.)

INVESTIGATIVE PROCEDURES

1. Ask the child what television program he likes best.
2. Now ask him to predict (guess) the most popular television program among (a) the other children in his classroom, and (b) the students in a fourth-grade classroom in his school.
3. Have him ask each child in his classroom what his favorite television program is. You can record each child's answer. Now, have him give each child in a fourth-grade classroom a copy of the questionnaire shown in Table 9.

Table 9 Simplified questionnaire for collecting TV data

Your name _____
Grade _____
Date _____
Please write the name of your favorite television program:
_____

4. Help him tabulate the data by putting the responses into categories. Table 10 shows the fourth-grade data that were collected.
5. Now help your investigator make a graph, using symbols to represent program choices. Let this symbol ⚥ stand for each vote for a favorite program. For a sample graph, see Figure 17.
6. Process the data for your investigator's room just as you processed the fourth-grade data—construct a graph.

7. Now ask the student-investigator to make some statements about the program preferences of the children in the two rooms, including the differences and similarities. (The activity of making inferences is treated in the next chapter.)

Table 10   Fourth-grade TV program data, collected from Room 4B

Fantasy World	///
Skip Williams	/////
Sparrow Family	///// //
Animal World	//
Those Sons of Mine	//
Lucky	//
Baxter Bunch	/
Football	/
Family Doctor	/
Cartoons	//

Figure 17   Favorite TV shows of one group of students

Review the preceding investigation for the primary-age inquirer by writing brief responses to the following questions:

1. What was the investigative *problem?* _____

_____

2. What were the *data sources?* _____

_____

3. What *data gathering technique* was employed? _____

_____

4. How were the data *processed?* _____

_____

5. (We will talk about inferences in the next chapter.)

1. *Problem:* How do the TV program preferences of primary graders and fourth graders compare? (Notice how Investigative Procedure #2 provided for hypothesizing.)
2. *Data sources:* All students in the investigator's classroom and all students in a fourth-grade classroom in the same school.
3. *Data gathering device:* Questionnaire.
4. *Data processing:* Graphs.
5. The next chapter deals with making inferences. However, notice how provision is made for this operation in Investigative Procedure #7.

A Processing Example Using Geographical Data

Take a few moments to study Figures 29 and 30 (pages 114 and 115), aerial photographs of a portion of the earth's surface.[1] For an investigator, the aerial photographs represent (check one):

_____ data gathering devices
_____ data sources

[1] For alternative possibilities for implementing the aerial photograph lesson that follows, see Arthur K. Ellis, "The Utilization of Aerial Photographs to Investigate Land Use Change," *Social Education,* **XXXIV** (Dec. 1970); and Frank L. Ryan, *Exemplars for the New Social Studies* (Englewood Cliffs, N.J.: Prentice-Hall, Inc., 1971), pp. 56–61.

The aerial photographs are data sources.

Which type of data source do the photographs represent? (check one.)

_____ primary data sources
_____ secondary data sources

The photographs are primary data sources, because they are a nonselective representation of the natural and cultural features of the earth's surface at the particular site. The camera's eye leaves out nothing that it can see. Any photograph represents, in addition, a compromise between the amount of area included and the clarity of the features shown. (See Figures 18 and 19 for an illustration of this fact.)

Figure 18 The camera is nondiscriminating in what it observes.

Figure 19 Close-up of the building shown in Figure 18. Area has been sacrificed for greater detail.

We can perceive the aerial photographs as primary data sources from which an investigator might gather and process data relevant to an investigative problem. If we used the aerial photographs in Figures 29 and 30 as data sources, which of the following questions would prove most fruitful as a guide to inquiry? (Check one.)

_____ 1. Who took the aerial photographs?

_____ 2. What patterns of land-use are evident, and what do those patterns signify?

_____ 3. What is the population of the city shown in the photographs?

_____ 4. What are the five white dots in Figure 30?

Question #1 merely seeks data. Questions #2, 3, and 4 offer possibilities for inquiry. See Chapter 3 to review inquiry-related questions if this activity was confusing for you. We have selected Question #2 as the problem to pursue further.

At this point we have an inquiry problem and a data source. Our next two steps will involve gathering and processing data from the data source, to pursue the researchable question: What patterns of land-use are evident, and what do these patterns signify? Let us begin gathering data. Examine one of the aerial photographs (Figure 30, page 115) and record in the space provided below any items of data which might help you answer the question: What patterns of land-use are evident, and what do those patterns signify? We have recorded a few items to help you begin.

DATA FROM THE AERIAL PHOTOGRAPH

River, farmhouses,[2] bridges, lake, highways, _____

_____

_____

_____

_____

Compare our list with your own: river, farmhouses, bridges, lake, highways, roads, streets, dam, railroad, stream, reservoir, houses, business area, school, woods, cropland.

Now that you have gathered some data from the aerial photograph (data source), let us consider two methods of data processing. The first method involves a classified listing of the data. Use the space below to list categories into which you could group the data you have generated from the aerial photograph.

---

[2] You may wonder why we list farmhouses as data. Your thinking may take the following form: farmhouses are not observable, but I do see structures that resemble homes surrounded by fields that appear to be under cultivation. Within such an interpretative context, you might infer that the structures are farmhouses. We do not disagree with your thinking. At some point the geographer, having observed consistent patterns for various spatial relationships, is willing to treat the inference of farmhouses as observable phenomena, and therefore as *data*. The determination of when students should be allowed inference–data jumps is probably best left to the individual teacher. Certainly the teacher can elicit from the student the basic data which lead him to believe he "observes" farmhouses.

_____

_____

_____

_____

═══

Again, our lists will vary. We came up with these possibilities:

a. Industry
b. Water
c. City
d. Countryside
e. Transportation
f. Words that begin with *f*
g. Words that begin with *s*
h. Words that begin with letters other than *f* and *s*
i. Three-letter words
j. Four-letter words
k. Words with more than four letters

_____

The categories we eventually choose will depend on the investigative problem and its interrelation with our frames of reference. We suggest that categories (a) through (e) are appropriate for our investigative problem: What patterns of land-use are evident, and what do these patterns signify? Try to process the data you listed previously under the following headings. Some items may be classified under more than one category.

INDUSTRY	WATER	CITY	COUNTRYSIDE	TRANSPORTATION

═══

It is important to note that your processed data list need not coincide with ours. The following list is meant to be illustrative rather than definitive.

INDUSTRY	WATER	CITY	COUNTRYSIDE	TRANSPORTATION
dam	river	streets	cropland	river
railroad	lake	houses	woods	bridge
	stream	business area	farmhouses	highway
	reservoir	school buildings	sheds, barns	streets
			land in the river	railroad

Besides categorizing the data, another procedure for data processing is *mapping*. To process Figure 30 from an aerial photograph into a map of that site (Figure 20), we must recognize the idea of *selective representation*. That is, (1) what things do we wish to represent as they appear in the photograph? (bridge, oil tanks); (2) what things do we wish to represent in a general way? (cropland, the city); (3) what things do we wish to exclude? (minor roads, cars on highway).

Examine the base map (Figure 20) which has been partially prepared from the aerial photograph in Figure 30. Involve yourself in this processing activity by finishing the incomplete map. Use the key and the finished portions of the map to guide your work.

Processing Data and Estimating Probabilities for Making Inferences

At the beginning of this chapter we reviewed the notion that investigators process data to help them make inferences. Let us now carry the activity of data processing a bit further. Consider the following investigation.

An investigator wants to inquire into the relative effectiveness of two strategies for teaching an American history course. The first strategy we shall call "case study–discussion." In this treatment, students are involved in a series of inquiry activities which make use of such data sources as letters written at the time of or about the Battle of Lexington (see pages 137 to 139 for examples).

The second strategy is to have students read from a history textbook, and to follow this activity with lectures by the teacher. This strategy we shall call the "textbook–lecture" strategy.

To determine the relative effects of the two treatments on student achievement, the investigator administers an instrument especially designed to test the content that was used in both groups during the eight-week dura-

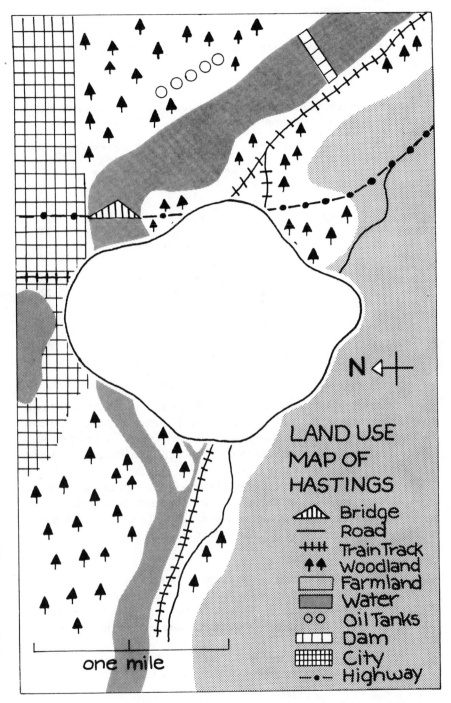

Figure 20 An example of processing the data gathered from Figure 30 into map form

tion of the study. Individual student scores on the achievement test are presented in Table 11.

Table 11 Individual achievement scores for two groups of students involved in different strategies for teaching American history

Case Study–Discussion Group Subject's Name	Test Score	Textbook–Lecture Group Subject's Name	Test Score
L. Anderson	32	C. Calvin	19
D. Bowen	17	R. Donald	22
A. Davenport	24	B. Douglas	21
A. Frost	35	L. Ervin	21
B. Gallagher	24	T. Ingersoll	28
R. Holmes	29	M. Jackson	22
B. Johnson	31	G. Keith	20
H. Johnson	28	R. Lewellyn	13
B. Lomas	21	B. Mitchell	19
C. Oliver	27	R. O'Rourke	22
J. Perin	27	D. Powell	23
R. Rivers	20	F. Riley	16
E. Stanton	25	E. Tong	23
D. Turner	24	B. Williams	14
D. Vincent	30	H. Zimmerman	19

In their present unprocessed form, the data suggest little about the relative effectiveness of the two strategies, and the need to process the data becomes evident. Earlier in this chapter we categorized TV program preference and bedtime data, as well as data gathered from aerial photographs, and similarly we could categorize the history teaching strategies data in Table 11. One form such a categorization might take appears in Table 12.

A cursory inspection of Table 12 reveals apparent achievement differences between the two teaching strategies. Using Table 12, check any of the following statements of differences that are warranted.

_____ a. More students received test scores of 24 or more in the case study–discussion group than in the textbook–lecture group.

_____ b. Over one-fourth of the students in the case study–discussion group had scores that exceeded the highest score received in the textbook–lecture group.

_____ c. Several of the students in the case study–discussion group scored no higher than they would have if they had been in the textbook–lecture group.

Table 12 Frequency of individual achievement scores for two groups of students involved in different strategies for teaching American history

Test Scores	Frequencies for Case Study–Discussion Group	Frequencies for Textbook–Lecture Group
35	/	
34		
33		
32	/	
31	/	
30	/	
29	/	
28	/	/
27	//	
26		
25	/	
24	///	
23		//
22		///
21	/	//
20	/	/
19		///
18		
17	/	
16		/
15		
14		/
13		/

Statements (a) and (b) have data support. However, statement (c) is unacceptable. Because no student experienced both treatments, there is nothing to support the prediction that a student who, for example, scored 21 in the case study–discussion group would have scored the same in the textbook–lecture group. If anything, the evidence presented so far would lead us to hypothesize that the student would score lower in the second group.

The history teaching strategies data can also be processed by computing the arithmetic *mean* for each treatment. Mean scores for each treatment can be computed by summing the individual student test scores within a treatment and dividing by the total number of students in the treatment (see Table 13).

Even though we have categorized the data and determined means for each treatment, we are still faced with this question: Are there any really significant differences between the mean scores for the two groups, or are

Table 13   Mean scores for case study–discussion and textbook–lecture groups

	Case Study–Discussion Group	Textbook–Lecture Group
(a) Total number of students	15	15
(b) Sum of all test scores	394	302
(c) Mean score $= \dfrac{\text{(b)}}{\text{(a)}}$	26.27	20.13

the apparent differences only the result of chance fluctuations among some of the scores? In other words, can we say with high degree of probability that one teaching method produced significantly better results than the other?

Employing Statistical Analysis

In addressing ourselves to probability questions, the role of statistical analysis assumes direct importance. For example, if in the history strategies study we had initially randomly assigned the students to the two groups (and therefore we could assume that the two groups were characteristically similar [3]), then a statistical technique called t test analysis [4] would probably be appropriate.

Employment of a t test analysis with our data results in a value of 3.87, which, referring to the appropriate tables, indicates that there were statistically significant differences between the study's two groups at the 0.01 level. This means that the probability is less than 1 case out of 100 that the statistically significant outcome was due to chance. Table 14 summarizes the results of statistically processing the data gathered in the history strategies study.

The investigator is now in a strong position to discuss and further develop inferences around the finding that achievement differences were statistically significant between the two groups receiving history instruction. He has advanced from a strong hunch based on inspection of group data (Table 12) and group means (Table 13) to a strong probability statement

---

[3] See Donald T. Campbell and Julian C. Stanley, *Experimental and Quasi-Experimental Designs for Research* (Chicago: Rand McNally & Co., 1966).

[4] For a basic explanation of t test analysis and other statistical techniques, see W. James Popham, *Educational Statistics* (New York: Harper & Row, Publishers, 1967). For more theoretical discussions, see William L. Hays, *Statistics* (New York: Holt, Rinehart and Winston, Inc., 1963), and B. J. Winer, *Statistical Principles in Experimental Design* (New York: McGraw-Hill Book Company, 1962).

Table 14 Comparison of achievement scores for the case study–discussion and textbook–lecture groups

Group	Number	Range of Test Scores	Mean Scores	t
Case study–discussion	15	17–35	26.27	3.87*
Textbook–Lecture	15	13–28	20.13	

* Significant beyond the 0.01 level.

based on the evidence of statistical analysis (Table 14) that the two groups in the study were significantly different from one another in achievement.

It is beyond the scope of this book to pursue further such statistical techniques as *t* test, analysis of variance, regression analysis, factor analysis, and the like. Our intent in applying the *t* test analysis to the history teaching strategies study data was to show how statistical procedures are used to refine the processing of data and to enable investigators to attach probability estimates to the inferences they draw from data.[5] The tie between making inferential statements from data and concurrently considering the probabilities that such statements are valid, is developed in the next chapter.

An Evaluative Summary

1. In summary, we can say that data are processed as (check one):

_____ a prelude to making inferences

_____ a way of stating an initial problem

2. We can also say that the way(s) in which an investigator processes data should be designed to (check one):

_____ expedite clarity of presentation

_____ furnish alternative examples

3. Finally, we can say that the specific means an investigator selects to process data should reflect (check one):

[5] See Frederick N. Kerlinger, *Foundations of Behavioral Research: Educational and Psychological Inquiry* (New York: Holt, Rinehart and Winston, Inc., 1964), p. 150.

_____ the nature of the data
_____ the investigator's purpose and capabilities
_____ the sophistication of the investigator's intended audience
_____ all of the above

1. Data are processed as a prelude to making inferences.
2. The way(s) in which an investigator processes data should be designed to expedite clarity of presentation.
3. The specific means an investigator selects to process data should reflect all of the above.

Check the items which are examples of processed data.

_____ 1. A map of the Hudson River Valley
_____ 2. A statement implicating the Emperor of Japan in the planning stages of World War II
_____ 3. A chart showing the production of automobiles by various firms during 1972
_____ 4. A categorized list of people's opinions of a certain brand of soap
_____ 5. The diary of a Confederate soldier during the Civil War
_____ 6. Computation of mean (average) scores for each group involved in a study
_____ 7. Use of a _t_ to determine the differences, if any, between the attitudes of boys and girls toward inquiry activities

The following items are examples of processed data: 1, 3, 4, 6, 7.

Data must be processed before inferences can be made. The nature of the data collected, the problem we are investigating, and the background of the investigator are among the factors that influence our selection of processing procedures. Frequency counts, histograms, and categorical groupings are some of the process forms we have introduced and applied in this chapter. We have also discussed the employment of statistical analysis to determine whether differences in group scores, or the like, are significant or merely due to chance.

Instructional Implications

We have emphasized that data processing is an operation in the inquiry sequence which occur just before inferences are made. We have also said that data processing can take a number of different forms. Additional data processing suggestions follow for your consideration. Although the following instructional descriptions highlight the processing operation of inquiry, it is obvious that no investigation could logically involve data processing to the complete exclusion of the other inquiry steps we have developed.

EXAMPLES FOR YOUNGER LEARNERS

1. Younger students might investigate numerous norms of behavior to gain insight into the workings of their culture. Such norms might include favorite foods, games, television programs, and school subjects. After they have gathered data on one of these norms, the teacher can ask the children to form a "human graph" to process the data. The purpose of the graph might be to convey the children's preference for certain games. In this instance, each child could stand beside a picture of his favorite game, and the teacher could transfer results to a picture graph, illustrated in Figure 21.

2. This example illustrates data processing by a group of children who had spent time examining a set of pictures of an Iroquois Indian village gathered by the teacher from a variety of sources, including past issues of the *National Geographic*. The children had received no information about the Indians except that which they collected by observing the pictures.

The children then used the data processing chart (Table 15) as a set of hypotheses to be tested against information gained from additional data sources such as stories, films, and textbook accounts of the tribe.

Table 15 Example of a data processing chart: Iroquois Indians

Food	Clothing	Shelter
Corn	Cloth	Huts made of dirt
Berries	Animal skins	Storehouses made of wood
Fish	Beads	
Roots	Jewelry	
Meat		

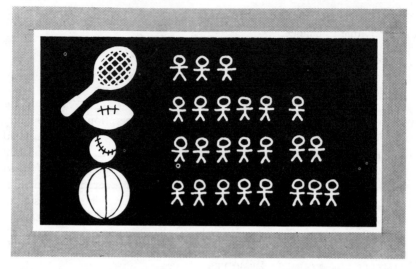

Figure 21 An example of how favorite game choices of students might be processed

EXAMPLES FOR OLDER LEARNERS

1. The map in Figure 22 is called an *areal coverage*. It records data which have been processed to convey the spatial distribution of public telephone booths in a nine-square-block area near a downtown district. Having posed a question related to the availability of public telephone service in this area, students outlined the street configuration for the nine-square-block field area. A team of student-investigators then began their field work by walking through the entire area shown in the map and recording the location of each telephone booth. Students could then glance at the resultant processed data (Figure 22) to determine whether patterns exist between the location of the booths and their proximity to other phenomena in the area, such as the intersection of streets, shopping centers, apartment buildings, and parking lots. Plotting telephone booths is only one of several possibilities. Shopping centers, apartment buildings, motels, garages, parking lots, "corner" grocery stores, traffic control devices, service stations, office buildings, and homes are among the many other phenomena that might be plotted and analyzed for patterns of location.

2. You can initiate another opportunity for students to process data by describing a "new invention" that might have market appeal. For example, describe a battery designed to power toy airplanes or cars,[6] an orange

[6] Lawrence Senesh, *Economics* (Boulder, Colo.: Social Science Education Consortium, 1966).

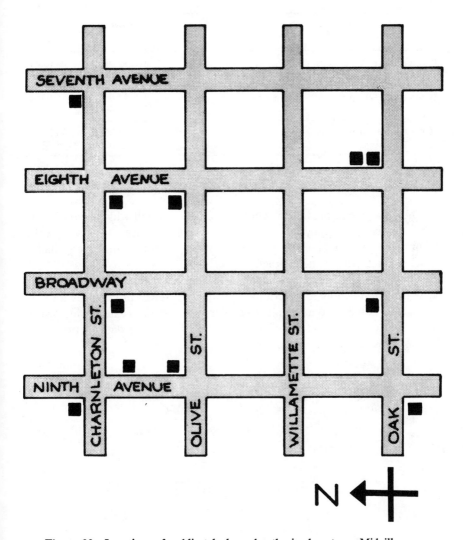

Figure 22 Locations of public telephone booths in downtown Midville

peeler, or a heavy-duty, high-security bicycle lock. Some students will certainly be able to propose additional ideas for a marketable invention. Suppose you describe a "new" bicycle lock, and you tell the students that the cost of producing each lock is $1.00. Ask each student to write on a slip of paper how much he would be willing to pay for the lock. The "sealed bids" are then collected and used to figure the margin of profit on various sales increments. Figure 23 gives some examples of how the data might be processed.

	Number of locks sold	Income	Cost at $1.00	Profit
If price is $1.25 per lock	2	2.50	$2.00	$.50
	3	3.75	3.00	.75
If price is $3.00 per lock	2	$6.00	$2.00	$4.00
	3	9.00	3.00	6.00
If price is $4.00 per lock	2	$ 8.00	$2.00	$6.00
	3	12.00	3.00	9.00

Figure 23 Example of a cost-products chart that students can develop

The next part of the lesson centers on a discussion of what should be the market price of the bicycle lock. Some students may argue in favor of the highest bid, overlooking the possibility of having fewer customers than a lower market price would attract.

3. Assume that a group of students has surveyed the student population at Washington School to determine the students' stated preferences for certain school subjects. Each student surveyed was asked to rate his interest in a specific school subject as either "high" or "low." The data as processed by the investigators appear in Table 16.

Table 16 Student ratings of four subjects at Washington School

	Spelling			Social Studies			Math			Reading		
	Boys	Girls	Total	Boys	Girls	Total	Boys	Girls	Total	Boys	Girls	Total
High	81	90	171	47	66	113	72	70	142	52	76	128
Low	34	35	69	68	59	127	43	55	98	63	49	112
Total	115	125		115	125		115	125		115	125	

	Fifth	Sixth		Fifth	Sixth		Fifth	Sixth		Fifth	Sixth	
High	94	77	171	58	55	113	80	62	142	73	55	128
Low	35	34	69	71	56	127	49	49	98	56	56	112
Total	129	111		129	111		129	111		129	111	

Earlier in this chapter we discussed the use of statistical analysis in helping the investigator determine the probability of the processed results being "significant" and not due to chance alone. If you wish to pursue this idea further, you might introduce a relatively simple statistical procedure applicable to the subject preference data presented in Table 16: the *chi-square technique*. W. James Popham [7] provides a very readable explanation of the chi-square technique and its application to data, and some groups of students are certainly capable of implementing the procedures he describes.

4. An alternative to having students indicate a "high" or "low" preference for each school subject is to have them rank-order their preferences. Here is an example of a ranking-scale questionnaire:

> *Directions:* Place a *1* before the subject you like best, a *2* beside your next favorite, a *3* beside your third choice, and so on until you have given a number to each subject.

_____ Mathematics

_____ Social studies

_____ English (language arts, reading)

_____ Physical education

_____ Art

_____ Music

_____ Science

Students can devise ways of processing the resultant data. One processing possibility is to sum the rankings awarded by the students to each subject. For example, suppose five students ranked social studies first, sixth, tenth, eighth, and third among all the subjects listed on the questionnaire. The same five students ranked mathematics second, eleventh, third, fourth, and first. The sum of the social studies rankings is 28 (1 + 6 + 10 + 8 + 3); for mathematics, the sum is 21 (2 + 11 + 3 + 4 + 1). For this group of five students, mathematics is more popular than social studies. The group of students could then offer possible reasons for their findings. We have found that this investigation pays off not only for students, but also helps teachers compare self-perceptions of their instructional programs with learner perceptions.

5. The purpose of this data processing exercise is to involve students in discriminating between statements of data and statements of inference. The data processing procedure which the students use here is a form of the technique called *content analysis*. It serves as a prelude to making inferences about the author's special interests and biases. To facilitate content analysis, the students could use a guide similar to the one in Table 17 as they read the following article.

[7] Popham, *Educational Statistics*, pp. 277–79, 291–300.

Table 17 Content Analysis Guide

Writer's name and position	Purpose of article	Statements of data	Statements of inference

Speaking Out on Our Schools [8]

Recently a group of kindergarteners was asked to give their ideas about reading and about school. When asked what they liked to do at school, 80 percent of those interviewed said they liked to do nonacademic things such as "play with friends" and "play games" while only 20 percent gave academic answers such as, "fix the clocks" and "learn to use the typewriter."

However, when they were asked, "What is school for?," these statistics were reversed and 80 percent mentioned academic things such as "learning to read," "learning to do things," and 20 percent gave nonacademic responses such as "playing."

All of the children (100 percent) said they wanted to learn to read but 80 percent of those children had nothing in mind that they wished to be able to read. Only about a fourth of the children had a particular reason for wanting to be able to read, such as, "so I can read to the little kids on the block." Furthermore, these children did not even know what reading was—only 35 percent conceptualized reading as getting ideas from words or pictures but most of them had undefined concepts of reading like "it's something a teacher says" or "when you're done reading, turn to page. . . ." One child said reading is "letters" but he didn't know what the letters were for.

What does all this mean in terms of how a child sees himself in the school environment? (1) Children must think that school is not for doing what one likes. (2) Although children want to learn (to read) they have no personal reasons for learning. This desire to learn must come from a source apart from the learner—probably the parents and the teachers. (3) Children are conditioned to want to read even though they don't know what it is and have no purpose for it.

Thus begins the process of forcing children to depend on schools and teachers. Children depend on their teachers to tell them *what* to learn, because the children do not understand what it is they are learning, and to tell them that they *want* to learn it, because they have no real purposes of their own. So long as teachers refrain from exploring concepts and purposes with children, this dependency will remain.

[8] Our thanks to Linda A. Miner, University of Minnesota, for writing the article.

6. A Gallup Poll on Americans' preferences for viewing sports events is presented on page 133. Have students carry out a parallel investigation in their school and compare their results with the national survey. In processing the results of the Gallup Poll, percentages were used and two categories, men and women, were employed. What are other processing possibilities that would add further insight into the results of the study?

7. The *t* test used to analyze the data of the case study–discussion and textbook–lecture study in this chapter could be used by many secondary students. Again, we recommend the Popham volume [9] for background reading. In addition, many university departments have invested in desk computers which are capable of carrying out various statistical techniques, including chi-square, *t* test, and analysis of variance. If such a machine is accessible to you, we encourage you to consider using it. Once the programs have been written, the actual operation of carrying out a particular statistical technique on the desk computer is easier than operating a typewriter.

[9] Popham, *Educational Statistics*, pp. 129–63.

7

making inferences

The inquiry operations we have discussed so far—stating a problem, identifying data sources, gathering data, and processing data—set the investigative stage for the main production: making inferential statements based on the relationships among the data. At this point the investigator can finally try to shed some light on his original investigative problem, and in the process produce new understandings and insights.

In carrying out inferential activity, we make a transition from being *data-bound,* as we report the results of our inquiry, to being *data-based,* as we discuss our interpretation of the results. The transition from being data-bound to being data-based can be precarious, if not disastrous, if the investigator is unfamiliar with the basic characteristics of inferential activity. However, let's get involved in the process, rather than continue to offer storm warnings.

Figure 24   Inquiry operation: making inferences

The Nature of Inferring Activity

Figure 25 shows the interior view of part of one room of a home. Using the figure as a data source, we could list the following data:

Four walls are shown, one drawn in greater detail than the other three.
A couch, lamp, lamp table, and clock are in front of the "detailed" wall.
Two pictures hang on the "detailed" wall.

Also, suppose we know that the wall shown in greater detail is constructed of wood paneling.

Figure 25 Partial interior view of a house (see also Figures 26, 27, and 28)

Let us now mentally remove the furniture and pictures from the room. Which of the following illustrations—Figure 26, 27, or 28—most closely approximates how you think the room would look?

_____ Figure 26
_____ Figure 27
_____ Figure 28

If you agree with most of the people we have asked to answer this question, you selected Figure 26. We shall assume that you did.

You have just been involved in an inferential activity. You quickly gathered the evidence you felt was necessary for making the inferential leap. You made the inference that because of certain data characteristics available about the wall, as well as other related data you could bring to bear on the present situation—(for example, walls are constructed before furniture is positioned; holes in the walls would defeat their function of providing protection from the outside; one rarely if ever sees a house with

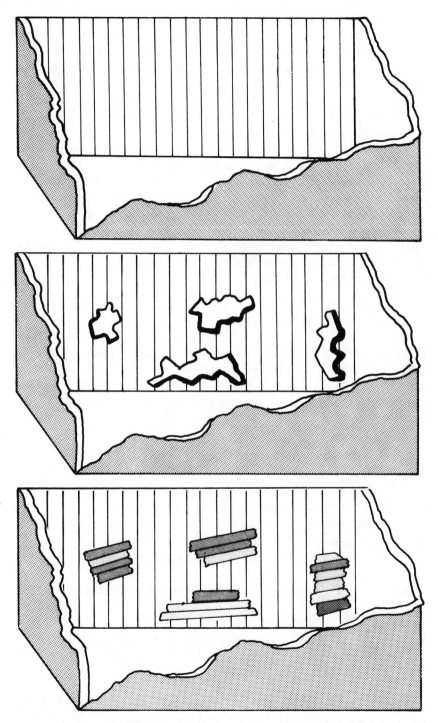

Figures 26, 27, 28 Which view is most appropriate for the house interior in Figure 25?

111

holes in its walls which match furniture locations)—you could "leap" to the pictorial statement that the whole wall is covered with paneling, even though it is not entirely visible to you. Furthermore, you probably feel that there is almost a 100 percent chance that your inference about the wall is correct. You could be wrong, but you are willing to take the risk because the probability of error seems slight.

Similarly, the scientific inquirer moves from the observable to statements about the presently unobservable when he has enough supportive evidence to decide with confidence that there is a good probability that his inferential statements are correct. Thus, the investigator moves beyond data to make statements based on those data, and attaches probabilities to his inferences. (Inferential activity is not always so simplistic as we have made it appear. Investigators sometimes disagree on what interpretations can be given to the same data, and on whether data are supportive or not supportive of an interpretation.)

The Need for Data Support

The potential for disagreement notwithstanding, let us again involve you in making inferences. In Chapter 3 you worked with a coin artifact. Examine the following list, which is based on observation of the coin artifact, and check the statements which represent inferences. (The coin is pictured on page 28.)

_____ A. There is a representation of a face on one side of the coin.
_____ B. The coin data tell us that these were deeply religious people.
_____ C. The words "We Trust the Gods" are printed on the coin.
_____ D. On one side of the artifact is a drawing of leaves.
_____ E. The people worshiped leafy plants as gods.
_____ F. These were peace-loving people.
_____ G. The face on the coin is a representation of the nation's king.

Statements B, E, F, and G are inferential—they go beyond the coin data. You probably recognized that A, C, and D are descriptions of data.

Now decide whether each of the inferences identified above (B, E, F, G) is sufficiently supported by data from the coin artifact. Opposite each inference, make a check in one of the two columns.

INFERENCE	DATA SUPPORT	
	Sufficient	Insufficient
These were a deeply religious people.		
These people worshiped leafy plants as gods.		
These were peace-loving people.		
The face on the coin is a representation of the nation's king.		

Although each of the statements potentially describes the culture we are investigating, none of the inferences has sufficient data support, if the coin is our sole data source. In a slightly different manner, you arrived at the same conclusion in Chapter 2. Review pages 27 to 31 and then return to this page and continue with the material that follows.

Making the Inferential Leap

Figures 29 and 30 are aerial photographs of the same site, taken seventeen years apart. As we mentioned before, aerial photographs are a source of data often used by geographers to study how man uses land. Below are three inferences. Using Figures 29 and 30 as sources, list the supportive data for each inference and then indicate whether you are willing to make the inference.

Inference 1: The town's population has remained approximately the same.

Using the aerial photographs as data sources, list the data that support the inference.

_____

_____

_____

Are you willing to make this inference? Circle one: Yes   No

Figure 29 Aerial photograph of a site (courtesy United States Department of Agriculture)

Figure 30   Aerial photograph of the site shown in Figure 29, seventeen years later (courtesy United States Department of Agriculture)

We aren't. Try to figure out why not. Write at least one possible reason for not accepting the inference.

_____

_____

_____

The photographs show only part of the town, and there may have been expansion in other areas which they do not show.

_____

Check at least one additional data source from the list below that would help you make inferences about the town's population.

_____ Census data for the town
_____ Aerial photographs of the neighboring area
_____ A globe
_____ Interviews with town representatives
_____ Coins found in the town

Appropriate census data would be most helpful. You might also use aerial photographs of the neighboring area, and interviews with town representatives, such as officials of the local Chamber of Commerce. [Note: Even though the inference is not initially supported, it could become a hypothesis for another investigation. We can think of hypotheses as tentative inferences that need additional data support, a point which we developed in Chapter 3.]

_____

Inference 2: Some of the farming patterns in the area shown in the photographs have changed.

List any data support.

_____

_____

_____

Are you willing to make the inference? Circle one: Yes   No

This time we are more willing to make the inference. Comparison of the two photographs reveals dissimilar field configurations (notice the contour plowing in Figure 30). However, the two photographs might have been taken during different seasons, during which different crops were planted. Such possibilities put in doubt our inference about changed farming patterns.

_____

Inference 3: Five oil storage tanks have been built (Figure 30).

List the data support.

_____

_____

Our interpretation of the photo follows: Five cylindrical structures are visible in the more recent photograph (Figure 30). It is difficult to use any of the shadows along the structures to help us estimate relative heights. The structures are located near a body of water that may be used for shipping. The inference that shipping is conducted is indicated by the structure which spans the width of the river to the right of the five cyclindrical structures.

_____

Notice how we attempted to establish relationships among the data, as well as among other inferences, in an effort to make an inference about the five cylindrical structures. We reasoned as follows: the structures might be storage tanks used in conjunction with nearby shipping activity. We were trying to tie our inference about the five structures to other inferences about possible shipping activity, evidenced by such data as the proximity of a body of water and the nearby structures across its width. We would have to evaluate our data support for these additional inferences regarding shipping activity.

Are you now willing to make the inference that these are oil storage tanks? Circle one: Yes   No

Although our interpretations of the data are possible, and maybe even plausible, we are not convinced that the *probability* of their being correct is high enough to make the inference that the five structures are oil storage tanks.

We hope you agree that the inference should not be made at this point. However, even if you disagree, continue reading the discussion.

We offered one possible explanation of the data relevant to the five structures. Now try to think of different explanations. One alternative explanation is that the five cylindrical structures are grain elevators. Use the space below to write at least one other explanation.

Some other explanations follow:

The five structures are missile silos.
The five structures are water purifiers.
This is a sewage treatment plant.
The five structures are gas storage tanks.

These explanations are not the only possibilities. You have probably thought of several that are not on our list.

It should now be evident that we need other data sources in addition to the aerial photographs if we are to make inferences about the five structures. List below at least two procedures for collecting additional data that would help us make inferences about the five structures.

_____

_____

_____

We could visit the site of the structures, interview people who know what the structures are used for, find additional photographs at different angles and at closer range, or examine topographic maps of the area.

Examine the photographs in Figures 31 and 32 and list the kinds of additional data they supply about the five structures.

_____

_____

_____

Additional kinds of data include the following:

Nature of surrounding terrain—vegetation, proximity to body of water, and so on

Some indication of the relative height of the structures

Indication of a possible connection between the pipeline and the function of the structures

Figure 31   A closer aerial photograph of the site shown in Figure 30

Figure 32   Ground-level view of the site shown in Figures 30 and 31

We shall not pursue further data support for an inference about the five structures. We hope that we have made the point that inferences are *supported* by data, and also move *beyond* the data. However, for those of

Figure 33 A source for closure

you who feel a need to know the answer to the problem, we have provided an informative data source (see Figure 33) about the five structures.

How Far Can You Go?

We have considered the nature of inferential activity and the need for supportive data. Next we shall explore to what lengths we can apply the inference we have made. Consider the following investigation: An investigator has completed a series of interviews in which one of his main questions was: What new car would you buy if you were to make such a purchase within the next two weeks? (This problem was first introduced in Chapter 5.) The interview data have been processed in the form of a histogram, shown in Table 18.

The investigator makes this inference: A majority of people prefer station wagons for a new car. In the space below, evaluate and explain your reaction to this inference.

Table 18   New car preferences

Percentage	Type of Vehicle

Percentage			
100			
90			
80			
70			
60			
40			
30			
20			
10			
0			
	Station Wagons	Passenger Cars	Sports Cars

The inference is too broad. Who were the *people* interviewed?

_____

Which of the following is the best inferential statement from the data on new car preferences?

_____ a. A majority of those questioned preferred station wagons for a new car.

_____ b. The majority of people in the United States prefer station wagons for a new car.

_____ c. The majority of people living in one city prefer station wagons for a new car.

We selected (a), because we know too little about the interview sample at this time to get beyond this statement. However, the other inferences are not necessarily incorrect; we simply are not yet justified in saying that they are *probably* correct.

_____

Now consider how the characteristics of the people sampled in this study might influence their responses to the question about new car preferences. We might surmise, for example, that age could be a factor, and that various age groups would have different new car preferences. Try to list three other factors that might influence new car selection.

_____

_____

_____

_____

Other factors might include sex, marital status, income, other cars presently owned (model, size, number, value), size of family, age of children, location of residence (urban, rural, small city, large city), extent of education, nature of employment, distance from home to work, and so on.

_____

Sampling the Population

Earlier in the chapter we made this inference from the new car data: A majority of those sampled preferred station wagons for a new car. Using several of the characteristics in the last frame, we can now refine our understanding about the people sampled. For example, our sample may have included only single men and women college graduates between the ages of eighteen and twenty-five living in a population center of 300,000 or more. It is important that we know who or what our sample *represents* before we make any inferences. In practice, such information must be clear to the investigator as he goes about the task of selecting data sources.

Sometimes you may want to confine your inferences to the particular sample included in your investigation. For example, you are interested in the TV viewing habits of first graders in your school, or the new car preferences of people living in Millbrae, California or Teaneck, New Jersey. However, investigators frequently want to generate inferences that are applicable to more than the immediate sample with which they have worked. They therefore investigate the TV viewing habits of various *samples* [1] of first graders, for instance, so they can make inferential statements about the viewing habits of *all* first graders who share the characteristics of those

---

[1] A sample is a small group which represents a larger group. For example, ten marbles drawn randomly from a bag of thirty marbles are a *sample* of ten from a population of thirty.

sampled. Similarly, a scientist tries a new drug on a group of patients to learn whether it will cure their illness *and* that of the larger population of patients with similar symptoms. In such a situation the scientist is saying, in effect, "I feel confident enough about my procedures to extend my inferences about those (people, things, phenomena) that were included in my investigative sample to those with similar characteristics that I did not study." Thus, the investigator is allowing a sample (or a series of samples) to represent many other similar samples that *could* have been taken, but were not. In research parlance, the investigator is studying a *sample* to make inferences about a *population*.

To recapitulate, an investigator may make inferences that apply only to his study's sample. But investigators are ordinarily interested in inferring to that population which they feel their sample represents. In either instance, the investigator must recognize the salient characteristics of his sample. It is beyond the scope of this book to discuss exhaustively the methods for drawing representative samplings for the purpose of making inferences from samples to a population. However, the following example might help you gain at least a partial understanding of that activity.

In Chapter 4 we described a study in which the investigator was trying to record fan reaction to a professional football game. Suppose that the investigator seeks to make inferences about fan behavior (for the purpose of this example we can remain vague on what specific behaviors are being studied) at (a) a specific stadium and (b) all football stadiums in the United States. With a cadre of assistants, the investigator stations himself outside one of the restrooms to pass out a short questionnaire that is immediately filled out by the fan and returned. Using the resultant data, the investigative team prepares to infer about fan behavior for the particular stadium in which the data were collected, and for all stadiums where professional football fans congregate.

Let us try to describe the sample included in this investigation. Who goes to the restroom at a professional football game? Possibilities include:

Those whose seats are near the restroom
Those who are not averse to using public restrooms
Those with weak kidneys
Those who drink beverages that require restroom visitation during the game

There is a strong possibility that the sample may not be representative of the fans in this particular stadium, let alone of those in another stadium. If the investigator wants to make inferences beyond the sample at the restroom, he must seek a more representative sample.

Who Makes Inferences?

You may believe that inferential activity impinges only remotely on your daily life. That is incorrect. Each of us makes numerous inferences each day (for example, "They must have money," "You're in a good mood"), and we continually receive the inferences of others. News reporting, which we might consider to be the end product of a form of inquiry requiring data sources, data gathering, and data processing, bombards us with inferences. In some news reports, inferences are derived from very small samples but applied very broadly. For example, we might read or hear an excerpt such as the following:

> Students were asked their reactions to their experiences in the new "open" school. Johnny Smith enthusiastically replied, "I've never learned so much in my life. This is the most fun ever." And Ann Jones excitedly added that, "In our old classroom (self-contained) I got bored. It just never was like this."

Although the above excerpt does not explicitly state that all students like the open school, the reader can strongly feel the probability that that could be the case. Certainly the interviewer did not ask the questions merely to determine what Johnny and Ann were thinking as individuals. Who are Johnny Smith and Ann Jones? Are they honor students? Misfits? Do they possess superior intelligence? How and why were they selected for the interview? In short, whom do they represent?

To summarize, we must be able to describe the characteristics of our sample in order to determine its *representativeness,* which in turn provides the guidelines for our inferential activity. Let us now consider three dimensions of inferential activity.

Three Levels of Inferential Activity

Earlier in this chapter you had opportunities to make inferences and to analyze them. We shall continue such activities in hopes that our efforts become more systematic as we identify and apply several dimensions of inferential activity. We shall consider three separate levels of inferential activity: (1) making data statements, (2) relating the present investigation to previous work, and (3) drawing implications. To facilitate an explanation of each of these dimensions, let us establish a data base from which we can make inferences, by reintroducing an investigative problem presented in Chapter 6.

Sixth graders at Jones School are investigating the bedtimes of students in one of the two first-grade classrooms in the school. The sixth graders collected and processed the bedtime data shown in Table 19.

Table 19   Bedtimes of first graders in Room 1 at Jones School

Bedtime	Number of First Graders
7:00	3
8.00	15
9:00	4
10:00	2
No Return	4

Level 1: Making data statements.   At the first level of inferential activity, the investigator expresses trends and patterns among the data. In other words, he states the results of the study.

APPLICATION

a. Most first graders in Room 1 at Jones School go to bed at 8:00 P.M.
b. All first graders in Room 1 at Jones School who returned questionnaires go to bed between 7:00 P.M. and 10:00 P.M.

Level 2: Relating the present investigation to previous work.   At the second level of inferential activity, the investigator compares the results of the study (data statements), both those that support and those that do not support his hypothesis, to relevant investigations, theories, bodies of knowledge, and other valid understandings. *Note:* The purpose of a study is to advance knowledge. The advancement of knowledge is attained by drawing relationships between existing reservoirs of knowledge and the results of the current investigation.

Let us now relate the data from this study (Table 19) to other knowledge. Suppose that bedtime studies have already been conducted for the other first-grade class at Jones School and for the sixth-grade class at the same school. The processed data appear in Tables 20 and 21.

APPLICATION

a. Results of our study (Table 19) are similar to (that is, supportive of) results we obtained from the other first-grade class (Table 20).
b. Most first graders at Jones School (Tables 19 and 20) go to bed earlier than the sixth graders in the same school (Table 21).

Table 20 Bedtimes of first graders in Room 2 at Jones School

Bedtime	Number of First Graders
7:00	4
8:00	18
9:00	3
10:00	0
No Return	2

Table 21 Bedtimes of sixth graders at Jones School

Bedtime	Number of Sixth Graders
7:00	0
8:00	4
9:00	15
10:00	8
11:00	1

Level 3: Drawing Implications.   At the third level of inferential activity, the investigator draws on the data statements (level 1) and relationships (level 2) and offers interpretive meanings for the results of the study.

APPLICATION

a. First graders at Jones School follow rules govenring when they go to bed.
b. First graders and sixth graders at Jones School are governed by rules for similar behavior (the rules may be self- or parent-imposed), although the rules may differ between the grades.

Schematically, we can represent the three dimensions of inferential activity on a continuum:

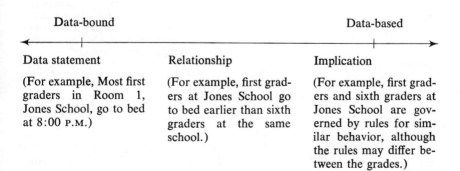

Data-bound		Data-based
Data statement	Relationship	Implication
(For example, Most first graders in Room 1, Jones School, go to bed at 8:00 P.M.)	(For example, first graders at Jones School go to bed earlier than sixth graders at the same school.)	(For example, first graders and sixth graders at Jones School are governed by rules for similar behavior, although the rules may differ between the grades.)

We make no attempt to locate the exact position of each dimension on the continuum. It is sufficient to say that the investigator makes a transition from being data-bound to being data-based in his inferential activity. At the beginning of this chapter, we noted that this transition can be precarious for those unfamiliar with the nature of inferences and how they are drawn. We now assume that you are not a member of this accident-prone group.

Table 22 summarizes the three levels of inferential activity and gives examples of the kinds of questions that can be posed to implement each level.

Table 22   The three levels of inferential activity

Level of Inferential Activity	Operational Definition	Examples of Questions to Implement Activity
1. Data statements	Trends and patterns among the study's data are expressed.	What are our findings? What can we say, using the processed data? That is, what are the trends, patterns, and relationships among the data?
2. Relationships	The results of the study (data statements), both those that support the hypothesis and those that do not, are compared to relevant investigations, theories, bodies of knowledge, and other valid understandings.	How do the present findings relate to prior research efforts? To relevant theories? To relevant experiences of the investigator? To other relevant information?
3. Implications	On the basis of the data statements and relationships, interpretive meanings for the results of the study are suggested.	What do the findings mean in relation to our life experiences and prior understanding? What statements can we now make about human behavior? About animal behavior? About physical and natural phenomena? What are the implications of the findings for existing practices? For existing programs? For existing theories? For further investigations?

Levels of Inferential Activity—
Another Application

Another example of the employment of various dimensions of inferential activity may be helpful at this point. One of the purposes of a study conducted by Frank Ryan [2] was to determine the effects of "advance organizers" on the achievement of fourth-grade students. *Advance organizers,* in instructional practice, are introductory materials at a higher level of abstraction, generality, and inclusiveness than the learning task itself. Thus, you might begin a study of the specific climatic role of Japan's main ocean currents by helping the students to (a) recall how the Pacific Ocean influences California's coastal climate and (b) perceive that the same ocean also influences Japan's climatic conditions. A main function of the organizer is to help the learner integrate new concepts with basically similar concepts in his existing cognitive structure.

David Ausubel theorizes that advance organizers provide an "ideational scaffolding" which facilitates the acquisition of new learnings.[3] Although he researched his idea with college students, he conducted little if any research on the effectiveness of advance organizers with elementary school children.

A portion of the discussion section of Ryan's study is reprinted below. Subheadings indicate the dimensions of inferential activity reflected in the discussion.

Data Statements—Trends, Patterns, Relationships Among the Data

Comparison of the mean scores for the post-test and retention test means indicates a maintenance of generally higher scores for the advance organizer groups in relation to the control group. However, the lowering of the F ratio for main effects due to treatments between the post-test and retention test must necessarily taint any interpretation of the effectiveness of advance organizers on student achievement as evidenced in this study. [Note: F ratio is relatable to the t test discussed in Chapter 6, but we shall not develop the concept here, because it is not germane to understand this example.] However, even within the limitations of such a framework of interpretation, there is evidence in this investigation that the advance organizers were able to improve achievement.

Relationships to Previous Knowledge

Apparently by employing advance organizers reflective of the students' existing cognitive structure on California's geography, subsumers were pro-

---

[2] Frank L. Ryan, "Advance Organizers and Test Anxiety in Programed Social Studies Instruction," *California Journal of Educational Research,* XIX, No. 2 (1968), 67–76.

[3] For example, see David P. Ausubel, "The Use of Advance Organizers in the Learning and Retention of Meaningful Verbal Material," *Journal of Educational Psychology,* LI (1960), 267–72.

vided for the subsequent reception of the more specific understandings on Japan's geography. The evidence is rather encouraging when it is considered that the programed materials themselves contained several built-in organizers through which introduced learnings were compared and related with one another. Learning materials so organized would be expected to reduce much of the potential pedagogical value derivable from advance organizers. Thus any indication in this investigation of the facilitative effects of advance organizers would be in addition to those aids to learning provided by the programs themselves.

Implications for Existing Programs and Practices

Recent unit guides of instruction developed for social studies classrooms in the elementary grades have stressed the development of basic concepts at early grade levels that are then expanded upon through succeeding student learning experiences. In the development of such units, it would seem plausible to include suggestions for possible advance organizers to aid the classroom teacher in formulating instructional strategies for developing the conceptualizations of students. Certainly the instructional problem of this investigation of using the students' prior learnings (i.e., California's geography) in developing new learnings about another land (i.e., Japan) is a very real one to social studies teachers. It would seem reasonable to expect that advance organizers would not only assist the teacher and the students in making a smooth transition between units of study, but could actually enhance the students' learnings in the "new" unit of study. In employing the advance organizers the teacher would (a) identify existing student understandings, (b) introduce the students to the subsuming materials (i.e., advance organizers) by (c) explicitly delineating the similarities and differences between previous and new learnings.[4]

Involving You in an Application

In Chapter 3 you were involved in an investigation of how the spatial distribution of the laundromats in a community was alike and different in the years 1950 and 1970. The following activity will use several of the inferences you made then, as well as others that have been added. You should now be able to separate the general term *inference* into the various levels we have discussed and to make applications accordingly. For each statement below, indicate its inferential level by using one of the following symbols: *DS* (data statement), *R* (relationship), or *I* (implication). You

[4] From Frank L. Ryan, "Advance Organizers and Test Anxiety in Programed Social Studies Instruction," *California Journal of Educational Research,* March 1968. Used with permission.

may find Table 22 helpful. The original investigation is presented on pages 32 to 34.

_____ A. Some of the newer laundromats are clustered near one another.

_____ B. Our finding that laundromats tend to be clustered near shopping centers is similar to the results of other investigations that have been conducted.

_____ C. People prefer to use laundromats that are convenient to other sources of goods and services.

_____ D. An apparent need for additional clothes-washing facilities has developed.

_____ E. Grant Street has more laundromats than any other section studied in this investigation.

_____ F. There were more laundromats in 1970 than there were in 1950 for the section investigated.

_____ A. *DS*
_____ B. *R*
_____ C. *I*
_____ D. *I*
_____ E. *DS*
_____ F. *DS*

If you mislabeled any of the statements, please reexamine the section on the levels of inferential activity. If you answered each of the questions correctly, congratulations! You are ready for the next chapter.

Summary

The activities of systematic inquiry introduced in the preceding chapters—stating a problem, hypothesizing, selecting data sources, gathering and processing data—allow us to proceed to the vital culminating activity of making inferences. We have emphasized the necessity of making inferences that are in harmony with the data sources sampled, and of having data support for our inferential leaps. Inferential activity can take place at varying levels of sophistication. We introduced and applied three dimensions: (1) making data statements, (2) relating a present investigation to previous work, and (3) drawing implications.

Instructional Implications

Each of the three levels of inferential activity—making data statements, drawing relationships, and expressing implications—need not be used in every inquiry experience. This is especially true in the elementary grades. For example, primary-grade students may find it easy to offer data statements, but may have difficulty with higher levels of inferring. Teachers should not be concerned, because data statements can represent a powerful product of student insight that has resulted from their imposing order on otherwise random events. For example, it is not new to the first grader that bedtime exists; however, his understanding that there is something systematic about this common experience is a powerful insight. The young investigator's discovery that "Most people in our room go to bed at 8:00" represents an inferential insight that imposes order that holds otherwise fragmentary events together, thereby facilitating further discussion of such concepts as "rules" and "power."

We have found that many younger students are capable of duplicating their investigative efforts in another classroom and relating the results to results collected in their own room. With a background of such inferential experiences, upper elementary and secondary students can be expected to make inferences at each of the three levels of inferring discussed in this chapter.

1. An excellent vehicle for involving students in making inferences is provided by the article describing the results of a Gallup Poll [5] of the interests of sports spectators (Figure 34). One possible sequence for using the article instructionally in a spirit of inquiry follows:

1. Present only the results to the students and ask them to analyze (that is, ask questions about): *the data sources* (who was included in the study? sportswriters? sportscasters? spectators at a particular event? participants?; what were the characteristics of the respondents? age? sex? marital status? income?; and *the data gathering techniques* (when were

---

[5] George Gallup, "Football Replaces Baseball as Top Spectator Sport," reported in *The Minneapolis Tribune* (January 16, 1972), p. 6-C. Used with permission of George Gallup.

Football replaces baseball as top spectator sport

Gallup Poll

By George Gallup. Director of American Institute of Public Opinion

Princeton, N.J. At a time when television experts are predicting that some 65 million United States viewers will watch today's Super Bowl game, the latest Gallup Poll reveals that football has now become America's number one spectator sport.

Baseball, a game long considered the major American spectator contest, has now fallen behind football as the game Americans are most likely to mention when asked which sport they enjoy watching most.

Today's results show 36 percent of all American adults naming football as their favorite sport to watch, compared with 21 percent who name baseball. In a Gallup sports survey reported in January 1961 the figures were almost the exact opposite—34 percent named baseball and 21 percent named football.

Basketball continues to be named the third most popular sport, but it ranks considerably behind both football and baseball in its appeal to the fans.

Today's results reveal that football has made its greatest gains in popularity with American men.

Basketball and bowling, however, remain more likely to be named as the favorite spectator sport of women.

Interest in football has no dobut been affected by the steadily increasing coverage the sport has received from the major television networks. Today's Super Bowl, for example, will be viewed not only by almost one in every three Americans, but it will also be relayed live to Canada, Mexico and Puerto Rico and via delayed satellite transmission to most of Europe.

Today's Gallup Poll results were obtained at a time in the year similar to other Gallup sports surveys, thus assuring that no sport would benefit from seasonal bias.

Today's findings are based on personal interviews with over 1,000 adults, 18 and older, conducted during the period Jan. 14–17.

Here is the question asked and the 20-year Gallup Poll trend: *What is your favorite sport to watch?*

Favorite Sport to Watch

	1972	1961	1948
Football	36%	21%	17%
Baseball	21	34	39
Basketball	8	9	10
Bowling	4	5	1
Wrestling	3	5	1
Hockey	3	3	2
Skiing	2	1	*
Boxing	1	3	3
Golf	1	1	*
Swimming	*	1	2
Horse racing	1	*	4
Other	10	4	9
Don't know	10	13	12

* Less than 1 percent.

Here are the results from today's survey broken down by men and women:

	Men	Women
Football	44%	28%
Baseball	24	17
Basketball	6	10
Bowling	2	6

Past Gallup International surveys have shown that skiing is the most popular spectator sport in the Scandinavian countries, while soccer captures the top rating throughout other parts of Europe.

Figure 34 Sports preferences of spectators

133

the respondents interviewed?; what training did the interviewers have?; how was the sample selected?).[6]

2. Have the students suggest alternative ways of processing the data.

3. Ask the students to use the processed data in offering data statements, drawing relationships among the reported results for the different years, and suggesting any implications of the study.

4. Have the students compare their inferences (data statements, relationships, implications) with those made by Gallup.

2. One decision which has far-reaching instructional implications and which in itself represents an inference (all too often made without sufficient data support) is the choice of a textbook or other material for classroom use. The ingredients of an instructional mix are threefold (teacher, learners, materials). We now ask you, the teacher–investigator–decision maker, to examine some textbook excerpts as data sources from which you will draw inferences about their respective potential as instructional devices for students' inquiry learning. We realize that there is more to choosing a textbook than an assessment of its inquiry component, but let us limit ourselves for the time being to that single consideration.

Your question is, What potential has each of the textbook excerpts presented below as an inquiry-oriented instructional device? From each textbook we present a portion on Columbus's exploration of the New World. View the excerpts as instructional artifacts which will serve as your data sources. Build your inferences from a carefully constructed data base. You may find certain data processing activities (perhaps a chart) helpful in building toward your inferences.

Excerpt #1: Christopher Columbus [7]

The man who discovered America was an Italian sailor, Christopher Columbus. He planned to reach the Far East, the *Indies,* by sailing west across the Atlantic Ocean. The idea was not really new when Columbus suggested it. Most people who knew anything about geography agreed that the world was round. Anyone could see that it ought to be possible to reach the East by going west.

A happy error. Most geographers believed there were nearly 11,000 miles between Europe and the Far East. Of course, no one suspected that two

[6] In an Associated Press story by Willy Grimsley, Baseball Commissioner Bowie Kuhn was quoted as saying, "We can do a poll, too, and get whatever results we want" (*St. Paul Dispatch,* March 1, 1972, p. 45).

[7] Gussie Robinson, *Man and Society* (Morristown, N.J.: Silver Burdett Company, 1972), p. 48.

huge *continents,* or land masses, stood in the way. Columbus, however, believed the world to be much smaller than it really is. He figured that the Far East was only 2,400 miles from Europe. Columbus persuaded the king and queen of Spain to supply him with the ships, men, and money needed to test his theory.

How strangely things worked out. The best geographers of the time were correct, and so they did not try the western route. Columbus was wrong, and he discovered a new world!

After more than two months at sea, Columbus and his men sighted land. The Indies at last, thought Columbus. Of course it was not the Indies at all. Instead, Columbus had discovered land that Europeans did not even know existed.

This was in 1492. Columbus made three more trips in the next ten years. It was several years before he and the Spaniards realized that they had not reached the Indies, but had found a new land.

Excerpt #2: Did Columbus Really Discover America? [8]

Using Historical Evidence. How do we know Columbus sailed to the New World with three ships in 1492? How do we know he thought he had reached the East? How can we be sure that these things are true? And how can we begin to answer these questions?

You have already looked at seven different ways Columbus or people who knew about him spelled his name. The letters and books people wrote about Columbus can give us some clues about spelling his name. Those letters and books are one kind of *Historical Evidence.* They are things we can look at and study when we try to find out something about the past— like the correct way to spell a man's name.

Evidence About Columbus. Another kind of evidence is a *journal.* A journal is like a diary. It is a written account of things that have happened from day to day. Columbus and his crew members kept a journal on the first voyage to the Americas. They wrote down what happened on each day of the voyage.

Experts who have studied Columbus agree that the information he and his crew wrote down in the journal was accurate. For example, they have found that some islands mentioned in the journal match those that really exist. These experts have also examined the directions and the distances in miles that Columbus wrote down. They are the same directions and mileage that Columbus would have had to travel to get from Spain to the New World.

You are now going to read parts of the journal kept by Columbus and his crew members. Can you use this journal as *historical evidence* to help prove something about Columbus' voyage?

[8] Allan O. Kownsler and William R. Fielder, *Inquiring About American History* (New York: Holt, Rinehart, and Winston, Inc., 1972), pp. 8–9.

3. Each day we come in contact with numerous inferences. These inferences are often communicated to us through the mass media in a way that strongly implies that the "results" we are seeing or hearing are representative of a spectrum of possibilities and have been derived from a systematic investigation. The excerpt on the open school, presented earlier in this chapter, is an example of such writing, and other examples abound in newspapers and news magazines. Students can practice isolating the inferences and then analyzing them for data support, representativeness of thought, and evidence of author bias. Other sources of inferences that can be analyzed readily include advertising (for example, a baseball player endorses an underarm deodorant, a movie and TV personality interprets a "study" of the effectiveness of various pain relievers, women discuss the advantages of a particular brand of detergent); news broadcasts (an "investigator" "samples" the citizen opinion on national priorities by interviewing the early-morning occupants of a Chicago train station); and textbooks found in the classroom (refer to the excerpts on Columbus in this chapter and on Admiral Byrd in Chapter 4).

The kinds of inferences we make are often a result of our personal frames of reference. For example, the stimulus word *car* probably evokes a different network of meanings for a professional driver, a housewife, and an eight-year-old. Similarly, a book on inquiry teaching may be meaningful to one group of teachers and threatening to another. The investigator who wants to make inferences about human behavior obviously faces a host of "control" problems that differ from those ordinarily encountered by an investigator studying physical phenomena. You can facilitate student understanding of such complexities by having them write history from different viewpoints, or even take the role of a historical character.

AN APPLICATION

Let us attempt to involve you actively in an instructional application that provides an opportunity for students to use data sources in making inferences. Suppose you are interested in writing an account of the Battle of Lexington, which triggered the American Revolutionary War. Below, list three or four data sources you would like to have access to while writing your historical account.

Possibilities include eye-witness accounts of soldiers and observers (log entries, diaries, letters written by participants in the battle, newspaper reports, magazine articles, reports filed by military leaders, drawings of the battle) and the accounts of nonobservers (found in history books and textbooks).

Now, scan your data source list and classify your selections as either primary or secondary. (You might want to refresh your memory by reviewing the relevant pages in Chapter 4).

Thus far, in terms of the inquiry model, we have identified a problem and discussed the selection of possible data sources. Of course, we don't know the items on your list of desired data sources, but we shall furnish below five documents [9] which are primary data sources. Read the data sources and decide how you might use their content (that is, process the data) to construct an account of what occurred at the Battle of Lexington (that is, make inferences).

Letter from General Thomas Gage, Leader of the British Soldiers,
to Lord Barrington, British Secretary of War

Boston, April 22, 1775

I wish to tell your Lordship of what happened on April 19. I had heard reports that weapons and ammunition were being stored at Concord. They were to be used by some troops who would act against our King's rule. On the night of April 18, I got some of our troops out of town. The leaders of these men were Lt. Col. Smith and Major Pitcairn. I did this as secretly as possible. Their orders were to destroy the supplies at Concord. The next morning I sent thirty-two more companies to help them. These men were led by Lord Percy. Lt. Col. Smith must have been seen because alarm guns were fired and bells rung. Some of their men fought off his troops. This took place within six miles of Concord. A few of these men fired at the front companies first. This caused our troops to fire back. That sent all the rebels running.

Letter from Joseph Warren to the Towns in Massachusetts

To all of us, friends who are ruled by the King. General Gage and his soldiers have begun to attack this colony.

[9] Adapted with permission from *The Making of American Revolution* (Cambridge, Mass.: Education Development Center, 1968), pp. 10–15. The documents have been rewritten at a simpler vocabulary level by Mrs. Renee Macomber, third-grade teacher, St. Paul (Minnesota) Public Schools. We have also had instructional success with taping the excerpts and letting students listen to the accounts, rather than read them.

On the night of April 18 some of the King's soldiers secretly came to Cambridge. Colonel Smith was in charge of them. They hoped to either take or destroy the weapons and ammunition that our colony had. These supplies were stored in Concord and were there to protect our colony. That night some of our people were on a road between Boston and Concord. These people were unarmed. They were captured and harmed by British soldiers. These soldiers seemed to be the officers in General Gage's Army.

The British soldiers came to Lexington on their way to Concord. Seeing these soldiers, the men from Lexington ran in different ways. The British soldiers ran toward them and began firing. Eight of the Lexington men were killed and five or six were wounded. The British soldiers kept firing. Only those who weren't killed or wounded escaped.

Friends, these are acts of cruelty against our colony. They are doing these acts because we and the other colonies won't become Britain's slaves. Now we will still do what the King asks of us. And we would still go to war for him, his family and his crown. We would give our monies and our lives to him. However, if he continues this cruel treatment we must fight against him. We pray that heaven understands why we must fight. We will either die or be free.

Report of John Parker, Leader of the Lexington Men

What I will tell happened on April 19 about one o'clock. I was told that there were British officers riding up and down the road. They were stopping people who passed on the road and saying mean things to them. I was also told that a number of British troops were coming from Boston. They were going to take our weapons that we had at Concord. So I ordered our men to meet on the Lexington common. There we talked about what we should do. We decided that unless we were harmed we wouldn't be seen or bother the British troops. When they suddenly came I ordered our men to leave quickly and not to fire. The British soldiers ran toward us and began to fire. They killed eight of our men. All of this happened without us even firing at them.

Diary of Lt. John Barker, a British Soldier

April 19, 1775

Last night six hundred men crossed to the other shore of Cambridge marsh. It was between ten and eleven o'clock. The leaders of these men were Lt. Col. Smith and Major Pitcairn. Only the leaders and a few others knew why we were doing this. As we crossed the marsh we got wet up to our knees. Then we stopped on a dirty road. There we stood until two o'clock in the morning. We were waiting for supplies to be brought from our boats. Most of the men threw these supplies away when they came. This was because the men had to wade in water that was up to our middles. After going a few miles we came upon three or four people. These were the scouts for the rebels so we captured them.

We marched until we were five miles from a town called Lexington. Then we heard that there were hundreds of people ahead. They wanted to stop us from going on. At five o'clock we came to Lexington. We saw between two hundred and three hundred people. They were on the Common in the middle of the town. We kept marching forward. We were ready in case we were attacked but we didn't plan to attack them. However, when we were close to them, they fired one or two shots. Our men rushed in without any orders. Our men also fired and the Lexington men ran. Some of these men were killed. We couldn't tell how many because they went behind walls or into the woods. One of our men was wounded but he was the only one. We then lined up on the Common. But this was very hard because our men were so wild they couldn't hear orders.

Report of Major John Pitcairn, Leader of the British Soldiers,
to General Gage

April 25, 1775

Sir, I am sending you this report since you wish to know what happened at the town of Lexington on April 19. I will briefly state the facts since I am very busy. Otherwise I'd give you a longer report of what happened that day.

Six companies of soldiers were sent to Concord by Lt. Col. Smith. They were to capture the two bridges on either side of Concord. At three o'clock in the morning we were within two miles of Lexington. Here we learned that five hundred armed men had gathered in order to fight against us. Hearing this I got on my horse and galloped up to the six companies. I went to the very front company. Two officers told me a rebel had left the others and come up to them. He tried to shoot them but the gun misfired. After this I told our soldiers to move forward. They were not to fire unless ordered. When I came to the end of the town I saw two hundred rebels. They were on a common and I came within one hundred yards of them. Then they began to file off towards some stone walls. These stone walls were off to the right of us. Our soldiers saw this and ran after them. I called to our soldiers not to fire. I said they should surround and disarm them. Four or five times I ordered them not to fire. Then some rebels jumped over the wall. They fired five or six shots at our soldiers. A man in one company was wounded and my horse was wounded in two places. At the same time five or six more shots were fired. These shots came from a meeting house on our left. When this happened our soldiers fired here and there. They had not been given any order to fire. This went on for a short time even though the officers and I had said not to fire. I won't tell you any more since I'm sure Col. Smith has given you more details.

Now, select any two of the five documents and write a paragraph describing the events of the Battle of Lexington.

_____

_____

_____

_____

_____

_____

_____

_____

Using the remaining three documents, write another paragraph on the events of the Battle of Lexington.

_____

_____

_____

_____

_____

_____

_____

_____

The following questions might help you and your students analyze the adequacy of this inferring activity.

How do your two historical accounts, using different sets of data sources, compare?

How do your accounts compare to those written by others drawing from similar sets of data sources?

What limitations must you place on your inferences because of the data sources you used?

What criteria did you employ for using some of the data sources more than others?

What additional information about the authors of these documents would have helped you in this inferring activity?

How do your accounts compare to those in various history books and textbooks (for example, *your* textbook)?

8

implementing inquiry activities in the schools

Throughout this book we have operated from a model of inquiry that includes five operations: stating a problem, selecting data sources, gathering data, processing data, and making inferences. The model we have used is not *the* model for all investigative activity; rather, it represents the sequence of implementation that investigators often pursue. For example, anyone who is interested in generating knowledge must at some point gather and process data from various sources, in a manner which is consistent with the investigative problem and which subsequently allows him to draw inferences.

Involvement in the inquiry operations we have described in previous chapters can help the student develop the "spirit" as well as the operations required to impose order on the seemingly innumerable bits of phenomena that form the flexible, changeable environmental cocoon around each of us. Inquiry teaching gives students opportunities to learn about the nature of knowledge. Literacy, as an educational objective, is expanded from the traditional interpretation—that of knowledge acquisition—to include an understanding of how knowledge is generated. It is the addition of the latter instructional commitment—understanding how knowledge is generated—that is a crucial, significant departure from traditional educational objectives. Historically, students have been asked to swallow knowledge and to preserve the wrappings in which it was presented. Thus, they passively consumed and seldom questioned the facts and inferences in various media such as textbooks, films, and teachers. That students could be producers as well as consumers of knowledge was generally overlooked.

Involvement in inquiry activities must not become a *substitute* for student exposure to the reservoirs of knowledge that others have generated. Instead, it allows the student to step back from his knowledge inventory and analyze the characteristics of what he has received. Inquiry teaching establishes a critical framework for analytically *processing* as well as receiving knowledge. We suspect that even the products of inquiry, because their generation has been examined by the learner-inquirer, have different characteristics from the "identical" content found in more traditional, non-inquiry programs of study.

The application of inquiry models to instructional settings can provide a meaningful framework within which students can view the relationship of their present inquiry activity to past and future activities. Thus, students can gather data within the perspective of having formulated an investigative problem and having considered the availability of data sources relevant to that problem, and they will also have an idea of the nature of the inferences that are to be drawn.

However, there is probably no process that cannot be pedagogically abused—not even the inquiry model. It might be abused by having students memorize the operations of a model, rather than translate them into personal applications, or by allowing students to conclude that following the sequential steps of a model automaticaly leads to the production of valid knowledge. It is probably the potential abuse of applying inquiry models to instructional settings that leads Paul Brandwein to assert:

There is a conspiracy of silence, as it were, when teachers try to reduce any of man's behaviors to "steps." Man's brain is a freewheeling association of impulses, a melee, a wind of thought and recall, not the stately procession implied in "process."

To press further by example, surely we clarify our unease when we describe a "method of mountain climbing" as follows: (1) select an unclimbed mountain, (2) organize a party, (3) plan the equipment, (4) climb the muontain, (5) plant a flag at the top.

Mountain climbers indeed do these things, but we are not helped by these steps to climb the mountain. To repeat, we know too little of the workings of the brain to bully its activities through a single process or a procession of processes.[1]

Obviously, memorizing a series of steps for mountain climbing does not ensure that you will successfully climb mountains. However, it also does not imply that realizing halfway up the mountain that climbing boots and a rope would have greatly facilitated the journey is rational behavior, or that scaling Mt. Everest is meant to be an exercise in "pure" discovery learning. Knowledge, whether about conducting an investigation or scaling the side of a mountain, evolves through the cumulative effects of the experience of others, yet it is always open to the creative modifications and additions of present and future consumers and producers. In addition, recall that in Chapter 3 we discussed the invalidity of treating the inquiry model as a series of fixed steps.

We have chosen to discuss the instructional implementation of inquiry in two categories: (1) applications of the complete inquiry model, and (2) applications of specific operations within the model.

Instructionally Applying the Complete Inquiry Model

One theme of this book has been that investigative activity consistent with the inquiry model can be implemented with students at the earliest grade levels. However, we may think of the characteristics of student implementations as varying along a continuum of teacher dependency, from *teacher-directed* at one end, to *teacher-independent* at the other, with a midpoint designated as *teacher-guided*. For example, below is a diagrammatic representation of how the same investigative problem—the TV viewing habits of students—is implemented differently according to varying degrees of teacher involvement.

Investigative problem: What are the TV viewing habits of students? (Introduced in Chapter 6.)
Data gathering question: What is your favorite TV program?

---

[1] Paul F. Brandwein, *Toward a Discipline of Responsible Consent* (New York: Harcourt Brace Jovanovich, Inc., 1969), pp. 31–32.

TEACHER-DIRECTED	TEACHER-GUIDED	TEACHER-INDEPENDENT
"What kinds of programs do you think students like?" "How could we find out what students in our room like on TV?" "I'll write down what you tell me." "Let's look now at our list. Did any students name the same program? Which one(s)? Count how many named program X" (one of the programs named by several students). "What kinds of programs do students in our room like the most? Is this what we guessed?" "Do you think other students would answer as you did? Why?"	"What are your guesses on program preferences?" "What are the reasons for your guesses?" "What techniques of inquiry could we use to collect the data we need?" "Which technique(s) shall we use? Why?" "Which tools for gathering data should we use? Why?" "What are some guidelines to remember while interviewing?" (Students construct an interview schedule.) (Students conduct interviews.) "What are some ways we can organize (process) the data?" "Which of the ways suggested for processing the data are the best for us? Why?" "What are some inferences we can make? How do our inferences compare to our previous guesses? To other studies we have conducted? To the results of the investigations of others? "What are the implications of our study for advertisers? For TV program developers? For future research?"	Students independently carry out the inquiry operations of the model.

One observation we made from glancing at the continuum for implementing the inquiry model is that in each instance the student is actively *involved,* but the nature of his involvement is influenced by the instructional role assumed by his teacher.

In general, we expect a progression from teacher-directed to teacher-independent implementation as students undertake succeeding inquiry experiences. Using grade-level designations, we can diagram the approximate nature of such an inquiry experiences progression as follows:

Nature of Inquiry Model Implementation	*Teacher-directed*	*Teacher-guided*	*Teacher-independent*
	K–4		
Grade Levels (approximate)		3–7	
			6–12

The main point of the diagram is that a continuum of strategies may be used for each grade level (indeed, even for each lesson), with an overall progression from teacher-directed to teacher-independent implementation. The specific grade-level designations should be viewed as examples, not as prescriptions.

Instructionally Applying Specific Operations of Inquiry Within the Model

We have emphasized that inquiry teaching consists of the implementation of five operations of an inquiry model. However, teachers may have occasion to emphasize specific operations selectively, even to the exclusion (temporarily, anyway) of other inquiry operations. Therefore, inquiry teaching encompasses student involvement with the operations of inquiry, either collectively, as presented in a model of inquiry, or singly or in various combinations. Listed below are several of the lessons described in this book that highlight student involvement with specific inquiry operations.

Hypothesizing, Chapter 2
Working with aerial photographs to determine land-use changes, Chapter 6
Reading data from a coin artifact, Chapter 3
Questioning the data sources used by the author of a history text, Chapter 4

Making maps from an aerial photograph, Chapter 6

Using questionnaires, observation guides, and other data gathering techniques and tools, Chapter 5

Inquiry and School Organizational Patterns

Many schools are now organized along cross-age, continuous-progress patterns which are well suited to the ideas presented in this book. For example, a four-member investigative team might include students of four different ages—seven, ten, twelve, and fourteen. If, for example, the team is investigating the TV viewing habits of students, they could collect data from several student samples and use more than one technique of inquiry. They could analyze the data in terms of trends in the various samples (Do older students prefer different programs from younger students?), and they could examine the effects of varying data gathering techniques (Do students respond differently in an interview situation than in a questionnaire setting?). Even the nature of the inquiry implementation (that is, directed–independent) could be varied among the team members. For example, the fourteen-year-old could serve as team leader and could direct and guide the other team members during the investigation.

Nothing precludes the possibility of forming identical-age as well as cross-age teams, whether in a graded or nongraded organizational structure. Even the most traditional programs (read, recite, and regurgitate from a book) could be significantly embellished if punctuated by two or three student investigations a year. Students could summarize their investigative activities around the various operations of inquiry we have presented, and could eventually compile the resulting articles into a student research journal.

Establishing an Environment for Inquiry Teaching

For inquiry teaching to take root, grow, and flourish among your students, you must establish a supportive learning environment. The spirit of such an environment is at least partially reflected in the attitudes an investigator must often embrace while involved in the various operations of inquiry. Such investigative attitudes are listed below, describing someone involved in the lesson which dealt with the events surrounding Admiral Byrd's alleged flight over the North Pole (pages 58 to 60).

Skepticism. On what bases does the author make his inferences about Admiral Byrd? What were the author's data sources? How reliable are the sources? Is any contradictory evidence available? If so, did the author consider and use it?

Objectivity. Until this investigation, I had thought that Admiral Byrd successfully flew over the North Pole. However, I must consider the additional evidence in the newspaper article and not let my previous understandings interfere with my examination of the contents of this contradictory report.

Tolerance for ambiguity. Because the evidence is contradictory and inconclusive as to whether Admiral Byrd actually flew over the North Pole, I cannot reach any closure concerning the event at this time. (Did you find yourself "needing" the closure provided by the photograph on page 121?)

Open-mindedness. My opinion is that Admiral Byrd did fly over the North Pole, but I am willing to consider and assimilate the arguments and supportive evidence of those who disagree with my interpretation.

Tentativeness of interpretations. I shall continue to believe that Admiral Byrd did fly over the North Pole as long as the evidence supports that position.

Free and open inquiry. Even though many people strongly believe that Admiral Byrd was the first person to fly over the North Pole, the event is always open to further study.

Respect for evidence. I must relate the content of the newspaper article to existing information on the events of Byrd's expedition. However, I must critically examine this "new" evidence before I use it.

THE TEACHER'S ROLE IN ESTABLISHING AN INQUIRY ENVIRONMENT

The teacher, as well as the students, must reflect the kinds of attitudes described above while the class is pursuing inquiry activities. Teachers are probably creating the supportive environment necessary for the implementation of inquiry activities when they do the following:

Are receptive to all ideas expressed, even those that are in disagreement with their own

Are careful not to suppress further development of others' ideas by imposing their own opinions

Assume that everyone can be an inquirer

Provide opportunities for students to share instructional settings, rather than filling every moment with their own rhetoric

Seek to involve each learner in all phases of any inquiry activity

Pose questions which require more than memory-based responses

Encourage students to supply supportive evidence and rationale when presenting ideas or taking a position

Serve as models for the inquiry attitudes outlined in the preceding section

Solicit many varied ideas from the students, as well as from other suorces

THE STUDENT'S ROLE IN AN INQUIRY ENVIRONMENT

Traditionally, students have been cast as passive assimilators of the findings of others. To create the appropriate learning environment for this passive student role, textbooks were passed out and the time-honored three r's of instructional procedures—read, recite, regurgitate—were employed. Seldom was a reading selection challenged, or the author's procedures for writing a book inferentially reconstructed and scrutinized. Knowledge was neatly packaged and presented to the student, and seldom did it occur to the majority of those consumers that knowledge is not a series of cut-and-dried ideas that have rolled down an assembly line for collection into bundles of absolutes. Educators have often made the mistake of labeling as "bright" the students who passionately consumed knowledge bundles (especially the factual variety), but who all the same failed to acquire a personal commitment to advance the frontiers of thought.

For inquiry teaching to flourish, the traditional student role must be recast. Students must be promoted from passive to active learning status, and must become questioners as well as assimilators of the findings of others.

A Closing Statement

The activations of the minds of student inquirers undoubtedly poses a threat to teachers who need the security of orderly lecture notes buttressed by authoritative textbooks. Certainly, the proposals we have made in this book can lead to anxieties as teachers try to anticipate the kinds of questions students might raise and the diverse interpretations they might impose on various phenomena. Possibly such trepidation is the price teachers must pay if inquiry objectives are to be achieved. However, we feel confident that such teacher anxieties will give way to renewed self-confidence and teaching interest, as successful inquiry experiences with students begin to accrue.

index of inquiry activities

KEY TO INQUIRY OPERATIONS

H = hypothesizing, stating the problem
DS = selecting data sources
G = gathering data
P = processing data
I = making inferences

Activity Descriptor	Page Location	Inquiry Operation Possibilities
1. Norms of behavior: bedtimes	7–8	H, DS, G, P, I
2. Enculturation: participant observation	8–9	H, DS, G, P, I
3. Plant growth: gibberellic acid	11–12	H, DS, G, P, I
4. List: potential problems for inquiry	12	H
5. Foxborough: TV	13–14	H
6. Smith-Johnson method	14	H
7. Dry Gulch: fastest route	14–16	H
8. Formal education: occupation	17	H
9. Chamber of Commerce: sports stadium	17–18	H
10. Spelling achievement: distraction	17–18	H
11. Questionnaire: favorites	20	H, DS, G, P, I
12. Cluster of 12 statements of problems	20–21	H
13. Chinese discover America?	21, 22, 23	H, DS, G, P, I
14. Forced choice: choices of colleagues	22, 24	H, DS
15. Forced choice: match words to describe human behavior	22, 24	H, DS
16. Coin artifact	27–31	DS, G, I
17. Laundromat: spatial interaction	32–34	H, DS, G, P, I
18. Puzzle	36–37	DS, I
19. Dilemma-centered situation	37	DS, G, P, I
20. Behavior specimen	37–38	DS, G, P, I
21. Textbook selection	38–39	DS, G, P, I
22. Pilgrims selection	39	DS, G, P
23. "Hunter-Gatherers"	39–40	H, DS, G, P, I
24. Aerial photos: data-inferences	41	DS, G, P, I
25. 4 maps of Country X	41–42	H, DS, G, P, I
26. Wallet as data source	45, 46, 47, 49	DS, G, P, I
27. Hopi Indians	48–49	DS
28. Primary, secondary sources	50	DS
29. Battle of Lexington: selecting data sources	51–52	DS
30. Battle of Lexington: appropriateness of one data source	53–54	DS
31. Football game: appropriateness of sources	54–55	DS
32. Using artifacts as data sources	55–56	H, DS, G, P, I
33. U.S. artifacts	56–57	DS, G, I
34. Admiral Byrd reaches(?) the North Pole	58–59, 60	H, DS, G, P, I
35. Coverage of present-day events	59	H, DS, G, P, I
36. Artifacts: fountain pen, et al.	59	H, DS, G, P, I
37. Word artifacts	59	H, DS, G, P, I
38. Time capsule	61	H, DS, G, P
39. Rating school activities	67	H, DS, G, P, I
40. Lake City car preferences	70–72	H, DS, G

index of topics